Understanding the Quran

The Quran's style, topics, arrangement, consistency, collection, transmission, and understanding of the selected passages as examples of the principles learned

Publisher: Ghamidi Center of Islamic Learning - Al-Mawrid US
ISBN: 978-1-966600-29-9

Address: 3620 N Josey Ln, Suite 230 Carrollton, TX 75007
Website: www.ghamidicenter.com
Email: info@ghamidi.org

Chapter 1

Introduction to the Course

This chapter introduces the course and its topics.

Introduction

The Quran is the ultimate source of guidance for mankind, preserved in its original language. Even though it presents the same message revealed to the previous messengers, its delivery style is unique. All scholars of the Quran agree that the Quran is a remarkable book, possessing a unique genre and style that cannot be compared to any other book in the world; however, many fail to understand its genre and style. Understanding the genre and style of this book is essential to appreciating the message and gaining guidance from it. Due to this lack of understanding, many fail to appreciate the Quran. They see the Quran as a book of disjointed statements, with no connections among the verses or between the verses and the Surahs.

This course covers various aspects of the Quran (without delving into its Arabic), including its style, topics, arrangement, consistency, collection, and transmission, which young students of the Quran must be aware of to gain a deeper understanding. Building on that foundation, this course will also explore various sections of the Quran as examples for applying the principles learned.

Course Objectives

1

Start appreciating the topic, style, genre, theme, and arrangement of the Quran when reading it on their own

2

Appreciate why the Quran is a unique book and how it should be approached when understanding it

3

Understand how the Quran was transmitted from the time it was revealed through the generations before it reached us

4

Apply the knowledge gained about the sciences of the Quran to the selected passages of the Quran

Structure of the course

- This is a two-part course, and Part 1 is on understanding the Quran.
- Part 2 applies the principles learned in Part 1 and covers Tafsir of selected sections of the Quran, titled "Gems from the Quran and Hadith."
- The brief descriptions of the two courses are given below

Understanding the Quran
Part 1

Covers various aspects of the Quran, including its style, topics, arrangement, coherence, collection, and transmission, that our youth must be aware of when approaching the Quran for deeper understanding. Building on that foundation, we will explore various sections of the Quran relevant to faith and different aspects of our lives and explain those passages in a style appropriate for teenagers.

Gems from the Quran and Hadith
Part 2

Building on the foundation laid in Part 1, this course will explore additional selected sections of the Quran relevant to faith and to various aspects of our lives, and explain them in a style suitable for teenagers. We will also explore various sayings of the Prophet and Bible passages relevant to the selected Quranic passages.

Learning the Sciences of the Quran

Note: The sciences of the Quran we will study in this course include its genre, structure, style, arrangement, and more.

- The Quran is a unique Book and the final guidance for mankind, following several Books that were given before and have since been lost to history.
- Its genre and style are distinct from those of books we generally read.
- Without understanding its genre, style, arrangement, and how it communicates with its various addressees, we cannot appreciate the message.

- By studying the sciences of the Quran, we will clarify and observe a few notable aspects of the Quran.

Common Misconception	In Reality
The Quran is a collection of disjointed verses compiled together.	The Quran is a highly coherent book in which the verses and the Surahs are tightly interwoven to deliver a meaningful message.
There are multiple opinions on who the actual addressee of a verse is.	Every verse has an addressee that can be identified
The repetition of verses reinforces the message.	There is no repetition in the Quran.
Need external sources to understand its meaning	No external source is need to understand its verses
Every verse is relevant for all times	Some verses and commands are for all time and some are specific to time, people and place

- The Quran is a book that exhibits complete coherence, consistency, and flow, conveying its meanings with absolute clarity and without any ambiguity when the verses are understood in context.

The Farahi School of
Thought
The 3 Giants

Imam Hamid Uddin Farahi
(1863 – 1930)

He is an 'extraordinary' genius from India, among the very few Islamic scholars who dedicated their lives to pondering over the Quran. For almost 50 years, Farahi reflected on the Quran, which remained his chief interest and focal point of all his writings. He is known for his work on Nazm, or Coherence in the Quran. He was instrumental in producing scholarly work on the theory that the verses and Surahs of the Quran are coherently interconnected. With this inherent coherence, he demonstrated that each verse in the Quran has only one interpretation.

Maulana Amin Ahsan Islahi
(1904 – 1997)

A Pakistani Muslim Scholar, best known for his Quran Tafsir, *Tadabbur-e-Quran* (Pondering on the Quran). Like his teacher, Farahi, he dedicated his life to pondering over the Quran. He took 22 years to finish his tafsir of the Quran. In addition to the 9-volume tafsir, he authored 21 books on various Islamic topics. What's unique about his tafsir is that he never went outside the Quran to explain it. He believed that the Quran explains itself.

Javed Ahmed Ghamidi

Born in 1952, Javed Ahmed Ghamidi is a Pakistani scholar, philosopher, and educationist of Islam, a student of Amin Ahsan Islahi. He founded the Al-Mawrid Institute of Islamic Sciences in Lahore, which is well-known for its Islamic research and education.

Besides his excellent Quran tafsir, Al-Bayan, his unique contribution is his extraordinary work, Al-Mizan. Al-Mizan is a unique book that describes Islam in its pure form, cleansed from Fiqh, Sufism, Philosophy, and other scholarly opinions from the past. He believes that God's Shariah is very limited and that one should avoid mixing human endeavors of understanding with God's Shariah.

External Resources

Annotated linguistic resource on Quran with Arabic grammar, syntax, and morphology for each word

https://corpus.quran.com/

Quran Tafseer by Javed Ahmed Ghamidi (Select English language)
https://www.javedahmedghamidi.org/#!/quran-home

Translation and Commentary by Abu Aala Maududi
https://islamicstudies.info/tafheem.php

Easy Quran Translation
https://www.clearquran.org/

Hadith Resources
 https://ahadith.co.uk/
 https://sunnah.com/

- What benefits do you want to get by attending this course?
- Have you read the Quran with a translation, and do you find it difficult to understand?

Admin notes

- You are required to attend all classes unless you have a valid reason to skip.
- Please send a note to your teacher (or ask your parents) if you will skip a session.
- Attendance will be taken at the beginning of every class. Arriving in class 5 minutes after the start will be considered tardy.
- Three (3) tardies will be counted as one absence.
- Attendance will be counted toward your final assessment.
- Every student will be assessed via:
    - Participation in the class
    - Multiple Quizzes
    - Assignments
    - Semester Exam
    - End-of-Year Exam

Chapter 2

Introduction to the Quran

This chapter provides a brief introduction to the last book of God Almighty, the Quran. The details will be discussed in the subsequent chapters.

The main source of Islam

- For us now, Prophet Muhammad is the <u>ONLY</u> source of Islam. For something to be part of the religion of Islam, it must be given or sanctioned by Prophet Muhammad.
- Prophet Muhammad gave us this religion in two forms, which serve as our sources and form the corpus of religious knowledge: the Quran and the Sunnah.
- The Quran is the verbatim speech of God and His message to us in text form. The Sunnah is the practical aspects of the religion.
- Both the Quran and the Sunnah have been preserved in their original form amongst the Muslims and passed on from one generation to the next.
- Generally, Muslims attribute the Sunnah to Prophet Muhammad, but we must realize that we did not receive the Quran directly. Prophet Muhammad received it and gave it to us, making him its source for us as well.
- When it comes to authenticity, once it reached us, there is no difference between the Quran and the Sunnah. However, the Quran is the verbatim speech of God.

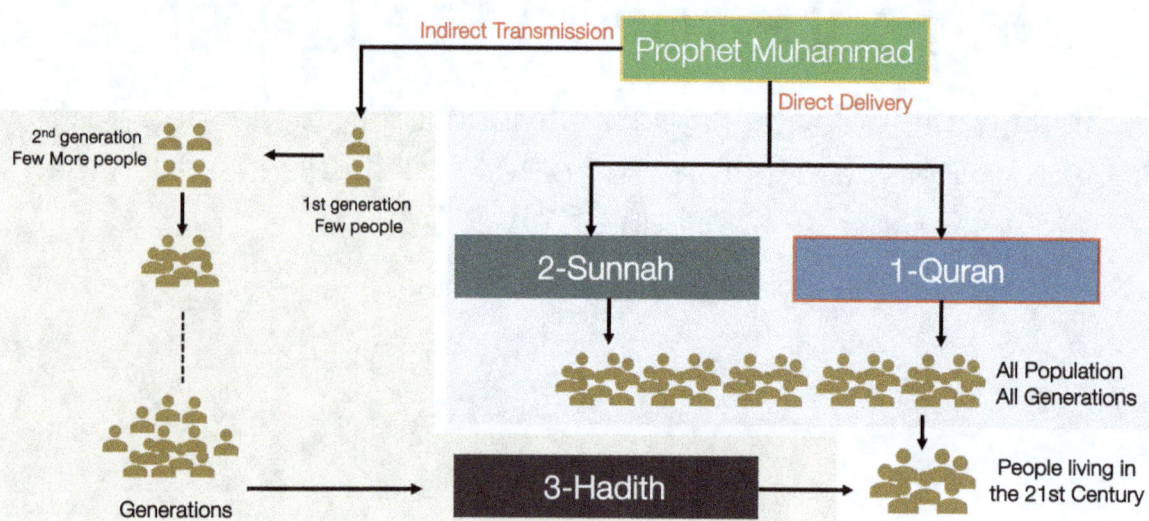

Hadith

Hadith is the historical record of Prophet Muhammad's actions, sayings, and approvals. It is another body of knowledge attributed to Prophet Muhammad. However, the method used for its transmission and preservation differs significantly from that of the Quran and the Sunnah, as shown in the picture. That's why Muslim scholars always consider Hadith as a secondary source of information about the main corpus of Islam.

The environment of revelation

- Knowing that the Quran was revealed in Arabic, which was spoken and written in the 7th century, is very important. The Quran was revealed in Classical Arabic, spoken in Makkah (Arabian Peninsula), in the 7th century (610-632 AD), by the tribe of Quraysh.
- The Prophet and the people around him spoke this language, but the Quran's articulacy and eloquence are inimitable. That period is called the 'Age of Jahiliyyah'. A clear understanding of the language of this period is essential to appreciate the message of the Quran.
- Some of the sources of the Classical Arabic language are:
  - The Quran itself (because it uses words in different contexts at different places).
  - Classical Arabic literature (especially poetry) reflects Arab culture and civilization.
  - Pre-7th-century history of the Arabs.
  - Ahadith of the Prophet that are transmitted verbatim (supplications and dialogues).

Walid Ibn Al Mughirah, one of the finest critics of language in Makkah, is reported to have said: "By God! None among you is more aware than I of poetry, neither battle songs nor eulogies nor the incantation of the jinn (charms). By God! The words spoken by this person (Muhammad) resemble none of these. By God! His words are delightful and lively. Its branches are full of fruit. Its roots are well-watered. It will definitely dominate [every other thing], and nothing will be able to dominate it, and it will crush everything below it." (Al Sirah al Nabawiyyah, vol. 1 Ibn Katheer)

Omar (RA) is reported to have said: "If you preserve your poetry, you will not go astray. People asked: "What are our poetic collections?" He said: "The poetry of the Jahiliyyah period, because it contains the tafsir of your Book and also the meaning of the words in your language." (Anwar al-tanzil wa asrar al-tawil, 2nd ed., vol. 3)

Religious groups – tradition of the Abrahamic religion

- At the time of the revelation of the Quran, the following groups were residing in the region:

Children of Ismail

Idol Worshippers: Due to greed and political rivalry, some people introduced idols into the Kaaba, and people started associating them as partners with God

Haneef: There were people among them who remained on the path of Prophet Ibrahim and Ismail. They used to be called Haneef (focused on one God)

Jews

They migrated from the times of the Romans and settled there, anticipating the coming of a prophet in this area. They considered themselves God's chosen people and considered their leadership role as their right instead of a responsibility

Christians

The powerful Byzantine Empire was ruled by the Romans, who spread Christianity to neighboring countries and tribes. Countries that adopted Christianity as their religion were Abyssinia, Yemen, Syria, and many Arab tribes.

The Quran addresses these groups and uses historical references drawn from the history they were aware of.

The Final Divine Book on Religion

- This is not the first book of Islam. This is the **Last** book of Islam.
- It's the verbatim speech of God in which not a single dot was added or removed by Prophet Muhammad – the only original, authentic, unadulterated, and trustworthy Book of God on earth now.
- Historically, scholars of various religions agree that the Quran is the only divine text among the Abrahamic religions to have been preserved and remain available in its original language. No other religious text can claim that. What scholars of religion debate is whether it is from God or not.
- Because the Quran is preserved by God, it calls itself "Al Mizan" – the Scale and "Al Furqan" – The Distinguisher. Which means every other text should be read and understood in the light of the Quran.
- Scholars of the Quran who rely on external sources of knowledge (e.g., history, the Bible, and the Hadith) when explaining its verses can inadvertently contradict the Quran. Since the Quran is regarded as the final authority, external texts should be interpreted in accordance with the Quran.
- A hadith might explain what's already implied in the Quran but is overlooked, and the Prophet Muhammad would explain it to the Muslims, especially if they ask about it or if an occasion arises.
- Its relevance is eternal:
    - Brings us back to our real purpose in life.
    - Keeps us focused on death and what happens after (the Hereafter).
    - Explains matters required for the spiritual upbringing of humanity.
    - Provides moral guidance
    - Teachings are based on knowledge and reason; intuition also bears witness.
    - Addresses human psychology and emotions
    - Brings dead hearts to life.

Quran is protected and preserved

- The Arabic language is a living language, spoken and written throughout the world.

- Since the time of the Prophet Muhammad, thousands of Islamic scholars have studied, practiced, and mastered classical Arabic.

- The protection, preservation, originality, and authenticity of the Book require divine intervention; otherwise, it will be lost over time.

> إِنَّا نَحْنُ نَزَّلْنَا الذِّكْرَ وَإِنَّا لَهُ لَحَافِظُونَ
>
> It is We who revealed this Reminder, and We shall preserve it (15:9)

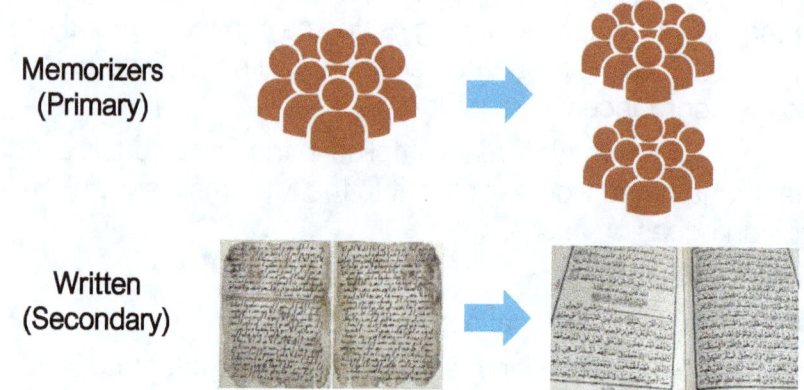

Memorizers (Primary)

Written (Secondary)

- This assurance was not given to any other religious text before.

Quran and other divine books

- It is a fact that other divine scriptures (Torah, Gospel, and Psalms) are not available in their original languages.

- That's why God called the Quran 'Muhaymin' over other divine books, meaning the Guardian or Protector. All religious texts and other Divine Books must be understood in the light of the Quran, provided the Quran addresses that topic.

وَأَنزَلْنَا إِلَيْكَ الْكِتَابَ بِالْحَقِّ مُصَدِّقًا لِّمَا بَيْنَ يَدَيْهِ مِنَ الْكِتَابِ وَمُهَيْمِنًا عَلَيْهِ ۖ فَاحْكُم بَيْنَهُم بِمَا أَنزَلَ اللَّهُ ۖ وَلَا تَتَّبِعْ أَهْوَاءَهُمْ عَمَّا جَاءَكَ مِنَ الْحَقِّ

And [O Prophet!] We have revealed the Book with the truth, confirming it before it and standing as its guardian. Therefore, give judgment among them according to the guidance revealed by God and do not yield to their whims by swerving from the truth revealed to you. (5:48)

Quran and Hadith

- The relationship between the Quran and Hadith is one of the core debates existed in the history of Muslim scholarship. To understand the message of the Quran and the relationship between the two, it is important to understand what Hadith is.

What is Hadith?

- Hadith is the historical record of Prophetic sayings, actions, and approvals.
- During the time of Prophet Muhammad, it was natural that the companions began writing down their interactions with Prophet Muhammad and recording them for their benefit. They used to narrate these interactions to people they met afterwards.
- This knowledge was naturally transmitted through generations, sometimes verbally and sometimes in written form (their notes).
- It practically turned into a body of knowledge a couple of hundred years after the prophet's death.
- Scholars then collected these texts in book form. For example, Sahih Bukhari.

The relationship

- As stated earlier, the Quran calls itself "Al Mizan" – the Scale and "Al Furqan" – The Distinguisher. Which means it is the scale and criterion by which all religious content must be judged. This includes Hadith as well.
- There is a common misconception that certain Ahadith supersede or contradict specific Quranic instructions, which runs counter to the Quran's own statements.
- Because if this is considered true, then there is no reason to believe that the Quran is the final authority, the scale, and the criterion of religion.
- The Quran is the standard by which everything else is judged as right or wrong.
- The Quran is a Furqan in the same sense, i.e., a book with the final and absolute verdict to distinguish truth from falsehood.
- A careful examination of those Ahadith that the scholars claim influence the Quran shows that they only explain or, most of the time, demonstrate what's already there or implied in the Quranic text.
- It is clear that when people were unable to comprehend certain stylistic features of the Quran, its background, and the implied meaning in specific verses, they also struggled to understand the Prophet's words on these topics.

Quran's Claim

اللَّهُ الَّذِي أَنزَلَ الْكِتَابَ بِالْحَقِّ وَالْمِيزَانَ

It is God who has revealed with truth the Book which is this scale [of justice]. (42:17)

تَبَارَكَ الَّذِي نَزَّلَ الْفُرْقَانَ عَلَى عَبْدِهِ لِيَكُونَ لِلْعَالَمِينَ نَذِيرًا

Blessed be He who has revealed Al Furqan (the criterion) to His servant that it may warn the whole world. (25:1)

وَأَنزَلَ مَعَهُمُ الْكِتَابَ بِالْحَقِّ لِيَحْكُمَ بَيْنَ النَّاسِ فِيمَا اخْتَلَفُوا فِيهِ

And with these [prophets], He sent down His Book as the decisive truth so that it may settle these differences between people. (2:213)

وَأَنزَلْنَا مَعَهُمُ الْكِتَابَ وَالْمِيزَانَ لِيَقُومَ النَّاسُ بِالْقِسْطِ

And with these [messengers], We sent down Our Book, which is the Scale, so that [through it] people can adhere to justice [regarding what the truth is]. (57:25)

Quran and Science

- While studying the introduction to the Quran, it is important to understand that the Quran is **not** a book of science.

- Some recent scholars claim that many scientific facts discovered centuries later are mentioned in the Quran. This idea is promoted by those who believe the Quran contains scientifically accurate descriptions of natural phenomena that could not have been known at the time of its revelation, suggesting a divine origin for the text.

- The details will be discussed in a later chapter, but it is important to note that the Quran is a **literary** masterpiece revealed to the Prophet, providing guidance on religious matters and conveying news about the unseen. Science, on the other hand, is the intellectual and practical activity that encompasses the systematic study of the structure and behavior of the physical and natural world through observation and experimentation.

Our Questions	Science's Answers
1. What is God's scheme for this universe?	✗
2. What is the purpose of our lives in this world?	✗
3. I have a unique personality; where does it come from, and where does it go when I die?	✗
4. What is death, and what is life after death?	✗
5. Which deeds are we accountable for, and when will we stand in front of God?	✗
6. How should one prepare for that day to be successful?	✗

Our Questions	Quran's Answers
1. Why is the sky blue?	✗
2. What is the universe made of?	✗
3. How do we get energy from the sun?	✗
4. How do we treat bacterial infections?	✗
5. How to improve the speed of a computer?	✗

Relationship between the Quran and Science

- As can be seen from the previous slides, the Quran and Science address two distinct domains of our lives and this universe.

- The aim of religion (or the Quran) is the moral purification of human beings so they can achieve success in the Hereafter.

- Science studies matter, the universe, and the laws within it – it provides answers to how, not why.

- The Quran alludes to various aspects of human nature, natural science, and history ONLY to substantiate its arguments.

- However, when the Quran mentions a scientific fact to substantiate an argument, it cannot conflict with the latest scientific facts (not theories), because the knowledge is said to come directly from God.

- Verses related to scientific phenomena must be interpreted literally, in accordance with the rules of the text.

It is not recommended to interpret science in the Quran or to interpret the Quran in light of scientific discoveries. Science is a progressive subject, and new research makes the older research obsolete.

Example of Quran and Science

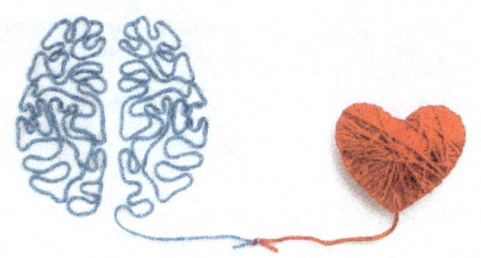

- Scientific research has established that the brain is the center of human thought. Similarly, it has been established that the heart is unrelated to the thought process.
- The Quran uses literary metaphors and addresses the hearts

- It uses the word "heart" as a seat of thought and the center of all our emotions and thoughts. This metaphor is common in many languages. We usually say, "My heart is not in it." When we are emotionally down, we say, "It breaks my heart."
- Can we say that the Quran is scientifically wrong?

Reference: https://www.sciencenews.org/article/new-3-d-map-illuminates-little-brain-nerve-cells-within-heart

If Allah protected the Quran, why are there so many "versions" (called readings) of the Quran, which sometimes impact the command of Allah also?

Chapter 3

Truth of the Quran
(Is the Quran from God?)

This chapter presents the case that the Quran is the Word of God.

Is the Quran the word of God?

Living in the 21st Century, the only sources of Islam are Prophet Muhammad and the Quran, which he gave us as the Book of Allah. Without ascertaining the truthfulness of the Quran and the Prophethood of Prophet Muhammad, we cannot be sure if we are on the right religion. Let's investigate a few universal truths that lead us to conclude that the Quran is not a human work and that Prophet Muhammad was a true Prophet of God because he presented this Quran to us.

Our sources of knowledge

- Three sources or mediums of knowledge shape how we understand the world, develop concepts, acquire skills, and make decisions. This is true in every field.
  - **Sensory perception** – it is the source of knowledge rooted in empiricism, the philosophical theory that all knowledge is derived from direct sensory experience. It involves using the five senses to gather information about the external world. Perception is considered the most direct and reliable source of knowledge because it provides immediate evidence of what is happening around us. However, sometimes, it can be deceptive.
  - **Inference** - the process of using existing evidence and reasoning to draw a conclusion or an educated guess about something that is not directly observed. It combines current knowledge with background knowledge to "read between the lines".
  - **History** - History is a source of knowledge because it provides an extensive evidential base for understanding how people and societies behave over time. The study of history is essential for understanding how the present came to be, as past events shape our current social, political, and cultural landscape.

Universal Truth

- A universal truth is a fact or a principle that is always true for all people, in all places, and at all times, until someone challenges it. They don't depend on someone's opinion, culture, or feelings – they remain true no matter what and are accepted by all.
- Some examples of universal truths are:

 The sun rises in the East
 All living things need water to survive
 Kindness makes life better for everyone
 Every action has a reaction

The process of deriving universal truths

- The picture below shows how we come to derive universal truths. To understand how we arrive at universal truths, start with the bottom-most layer: our sensory perception, and go upwards.

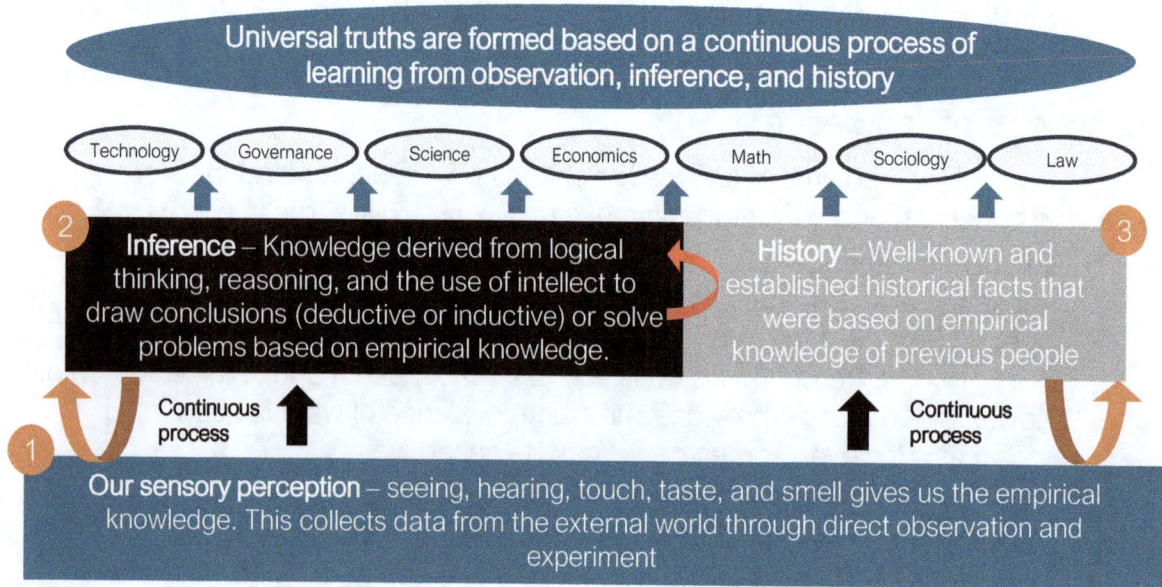

General Examples

Universal Truths	Source
Water maintains its level	Empirical
World War II occurred	Established history
Earth revolves around the sun	Empirical, Inference
A baby takes 6-9 months in a mother's womb to be born	Empirical
The universe is expanding	Empirical, Inference
The universe started at some point in time	Inference
All matter is formed of atoms and atoms are made of sub-atomic particles	Empirical, Inference
All crows are black	Empirical, Inference
Greece was the center of Western Philosophy	Established history
Socrates is the father of Western Philosophy	Established history

Some specific examples of universal truths

- Some specific examples of universal truths are shown here to make the case for Prophet Muhammad and the Quran. Let's review them.

Universal Truths	Source
An author who claims to write or present a high-quality scholarly work or book develops their thoughts and ideas from a young age.	Empirical, established history
Every book or writing has an age. After 100 or so years, it loses its relevance because human civilization, thoughts, ideas, various types of science, and discoveries progress, and it becomes only a great piece of historical work.	Empirical, established history
A book written over a couple of decades must go through a development, correction, and editing process before a final version is made available.	Empirical, established history
A book written over more than two decades without any development or editing will contain internal conflicts in its thoughts, ideas, and events.	Empirical, Inference
A person who challenges a powerful existing system with the support of only a few hundred people behind him never claims early on that in a few years, he and his supporters will be ruling the entire region over all the powerful nations around him.	Established history
A person who has never written an academic work cannot suddenly produce a high-quality scholarly work.	Empirical, inference, established history
A large book claims it will be protected forever, become easy to memorize, and be memorized by millions of people, cover to cover.	Empirical, established history

Now, let's look at some of the facts about the Quran and Prophet Muhammad in the light of the universal truths we just learned

Fact #1: No development in thoughts and ideas

- There is no sign in Prophet Muhammad's life that he **ever** went through the development of any of the thoughts and ideas presented in the Quran.

قُل لَّوْ شَاءَ اللَّهُ مَا تَلَوْتُهُ عَلَيْكُمْ وَلَا أَدْرَاكُم بِهِ ۖ فَقَدْ لَبِثْتُ فِيكُمْ عُمُرًا مِّن قَبْلِهِ ۚ أَفَلَا تَعْقِلُونَ

Tell them: "Had God pleased, I would never have recited this Quran to you, nor would He have made you aware of it. [It is His decision] because I have spent a lifetime among you (have you ever seen me writing or saying such a thing before). Do you not use your senses?" (10:16)

- The Quran is an ageless book. After 1455 years, it hasn't lost its relevance, even as human civilization, ideas, various sciences, and discoveries have made significant progress. Muslims still benefit from it to this day. It is still considered the center and focus of Islam.

Fact #2: No Contradictions in the Quran

- The Quran was revealed over a period of more than 23 years. Prophet Muhammad and his companions memorized it as it was revealed, without any editing. Even when it was written, it never underwent any editing. Still, it is free of internal contradictions in its thoughts, ideas, and events.

اَفَلَا يَتَدَبَّرُونَ الْقُرْآنَ ۚ وَ لَوْ كَانَ مِنْ عِنْدِ غَيْرِ اللهِ لَوَجَدُوا فِيهِ اخْتِلَافًا كَثِيرًا

Do these people not ponder the Quran? Had it been from someone other than God, they would have found many (internal) contradictions in it. (Nisa: 82)

- The Quran was completed and written in 632 AD. Nothing in the Quran contradicts or conflicts with any facts associated with other sciences from that time until today.

وَ اِنَّهُ لَكِتٰبٌ عَزِيزٌ لَّا يَأْتِيهِ الْبَاطِلُ مِن بَيْنِ يَدَيْهِ وَلَا مِنْ خَلْفِهِ ۖ تَنزِيلٌ مِّنْ حَكِيمٍ حَمِيدٍ

In reality, this is a lofty Book. Wrong can neither enter it from its front (in the future) nor behind (in the history). It is revealed comprehensively from the Being, Who is an embodiment of wisdom and has praiseworthy attributes. (Fussilat: 42)

Fact #3: He was not a writer or author

- Prophet Muhammad did not know how to read or write academically before he presented the Quran. There were many poets and writers at that time, but he never uttered a single word before the Quran.

وَمَا كُنتَ تَتْلُو مِن قَبْلِهِ مِن كِتَابٍ وَلَا تَخُطُّهُ بِيَمِينِكَ ۖ إِذًا لَّارْتَابَ الْمُبْطِلُونَ

And, O Muhammad, you did not recite any book before this or write one with
your right hand. Had this been the case, these disbelievers may get into doubts
(Ankabut:48)

Fact #4: God protected the Quran

- The Quran states that God will protect this book until the Day of Judgment. The Quran, a 600+ page book, is the most memorized book in the world since the time of Prophet Muhammad. Kids as young as five (5) years old have memorized it cover-to-cover.

إِنَّا نَحْنُ نَزَّلْنَا الذِّكْرَ وَإِنَّا لَهُ لَحَافِظُونَ

It is Us who revealed this Reminder (Quran), and We
shall preserve it (Raad:9)

Fact #5: Quran predicted his dominance early on

- Prophet Muhammad challenged the most powerful religious systems (Makkah was the hub of idol worship, and other neighboring powers were Christians and Fire Worshipers) with the support of only 10-20 people behind him.
- The Quran announced very early on that, in a few years, Islam would rule the entire region, subjugate all powerful nations around it, and dominate all other religions in that area.

هُوَ الَّذِیْ اَرْسَلَ رَسُوْلَهٗ بِالْهُدٰی وَ دِیْنِ الْحَقِّ لِیُظْهِرَهٗ عَلَی الدِّیْنِ كُلِّهٖ ۗ وَ كَفٰی بِاللّٰهِ شَهِیْدًا

He has sent His Messenger with guidance and the true religion so that it will
prevail over all other religions. God is a Sufficient witness to this Truth. (Fath:28)

In less than 100 years, Muslims were
ruling pretty much in the entire civilized
world

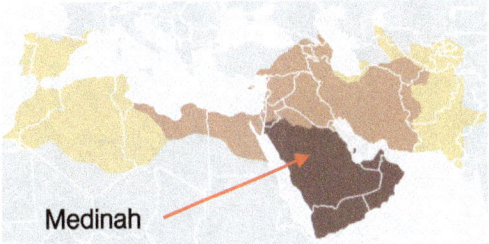

Medinah

In this course, we will learn about the Quran. Before doing that, why is it first important to analyze whether the Quran is the book of God?

Chapter 4

The Style of the Quran

In this chapter, we will discuss the style of the Quran as a book and why it is unique.

The Style of the Quran

The Genre of the Quran

- Scholars of Islam and Arabic consider the Quran a literary masterpiece with no parallel in human literature.
- By understanding the genre of the Quran, we can experience God by appreciating how He speaks to human beings.
- Some unique things about the Quran:
    - It has the beat, rhythm, and poise of poetry, yet it is not poetry.
    - It has the simplicity and continuity found in prose, yet it is not prose.
    - There are no chapters or sections like those in most books.
    - The people of Arabia likened it to rhymed prose, but with uncertainty.
- The Quran resembles (cannot be called strictly) an oration or a sermon given by a powerful Orator.
- However, scholars of the Quran unanimously agree that it is difficult to determine its exact genre.

> At best, we can say it's a powerful speech by a Mighty Orator

Dialogues in the Quran

- The Quran also contains dialogues between real characters of the 7th-century Arabia, very similar to a book of dialogues, and God is the author of these dialogues.
- Simple examples of similar works: Dialogues of Plato, Dante's Divine Comedy.
- The scene and acts change frequently, bringing one or more characters onstage, signaling a shift in the discourse.
- Words commonly used: *Qaala* قال (He said), *Qaalat* قالت (She said), *Qaalu* قالوا (they said), Ya Ayyu يا أيُّها (O ..).
- The speaker and the addressee in these dialogues are determined by the occasion and context (unlike in worldly books, where the author writes the names).

وَ تَفَقَّدَ الطَّيْرَ فَقَالَ مَا لِيَ لَا أَرَى الْهُدْهُدَ ۖ أَمْ كَانَ مِنَ الْغَآئِبِيْنَ

لَأُعَذِّبَنَّهُ عَذَابًا شَدِيْدًا أَوْ لَاأَذْبَحَنَّهُ أَوْ لَيَأْتِيَنِّى بِسُلْطَانٍ مُّبِيْنٍ

فَمَكَثَ غَيْرَ بَعِيْدٍ فَقَالَ أَحَطتُّ بِمَا لَمْ تُحِطْ بِهِ وَ جِئْتُكَ مِنْ سَبَاٍ بِنَبَاٍ يَّقِيْنٍ

He (Suleiman) inspected the birds and said: "What is the matter that I see, not the hoopoe? Or is he among the absentees? "I will surely punish him with severe torment or slaughter him unless he brings me a clear reason (for the absence)." But the hoopoe stayed not long; he (came up and) said:

"I have grasped (the knowledge of a thing) which you have not grasped, and I have come to you from Saba' (Sheba) with accurate news.

(Surah Naml: 20-22)

The statement suggests that this must be said by the bird

Rhymes and Rhythms

- The Quran's poetic style and rhythmic recitation are pleasing to the ears of every listener.
- Since it is not poetry, many linguists consider the rhyming system of the Quran as "rhymed prose ."
- The ending sound changes multiple times when the topic changes.
- It still delivers the message with complete clarity and without ambiguity.
- It is encouraged to read the Quran rhythmically.

"Beautify the Quran with your voices." Sunan Abi Dawud #1468

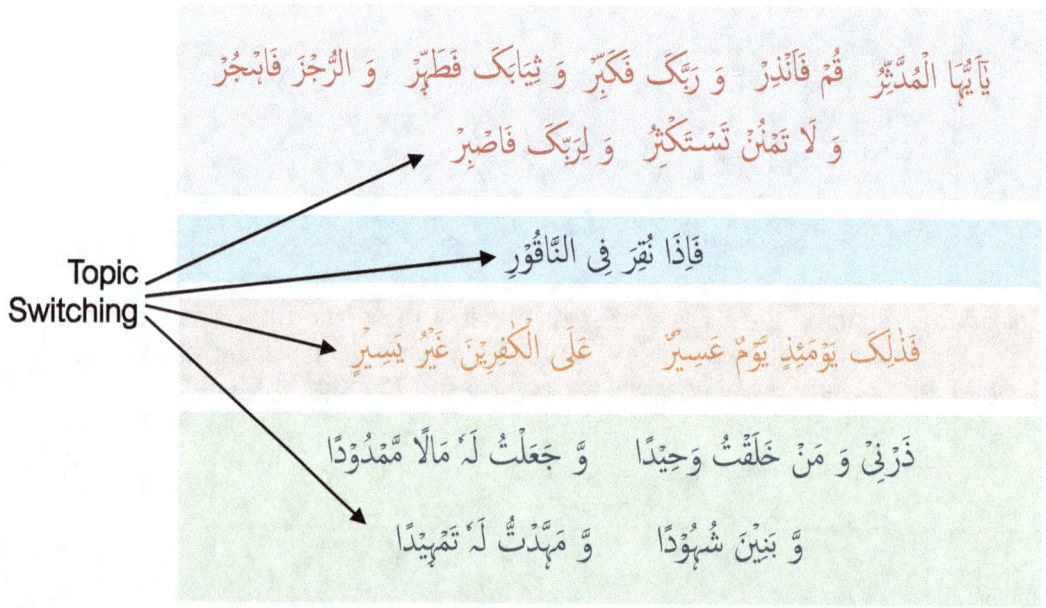

Narratives and Stories

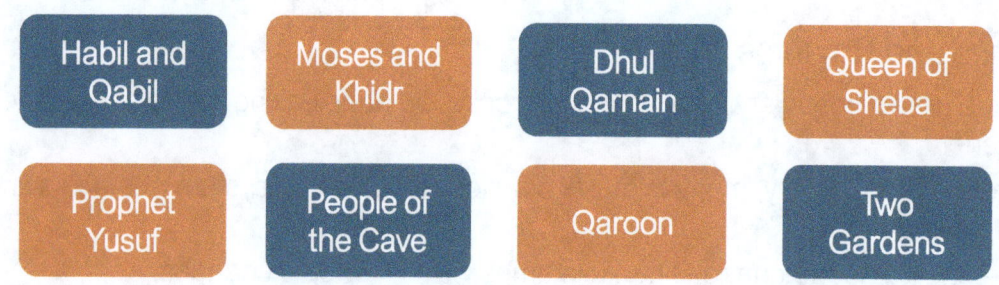

- Stories and narrations have always been an essential part of human connection, as they help people derive lessons and meaning from others' experiences.
- The Quran narrates many historical accounts of past events.
- One of the purposes of the stories in the Quran is to remind the Prophet and the believers of the past messengers and their companions, and to console and strengthen their faith.
- Some stories were repeated multiple times with different details depending on the context.
- The stories of the previous nations and their destruction are given to warn the people of Makkah about the consequences of rejecting the Messenger.

Similes / Allegories

- The Quran also employs similes in certain instances to illustrate specific facts or truths or to emphasize critical points in its message.

- The Quran uses many similes and allegories to effectively communicate complex, abstract religious concepts (especially related to Tauheed), making them understandable and relatable to people with varying levels of comprehension.

- They help explain non-perceptual facts by comparing them to perceptible, well-known events or objects, bringing these facts to mind in simple, fluent language.

اَلَمْ تَرَ كَيْفَ ضَرَبَ اللهُ مَثَلًا كَلِمَةً طَيِّبَةً كَشَجَرَةٍ طَيِّبَةٍ اَصْلُهَا ثَابِتٌ وَّ فَرْعُهَا فِى السَّمَآءِ

تُؤْتِىٓ اُكُلَهَا كُلَّ حِيْنٍ بِاِذْنِ رَبِّهَا ۗ وَ يَضْرِبُ اللهُ الْاَمْثَالَ لِلنَّاسِ لَعَلَّهُمْ يَتَذَكَّرُوْنَ

وَ مَثَلُ كَلِمَةٍ خَبِيْثَةٍ كَشَجَرَةٍ خَبِيْثَةِ اجْتُثَّتْ مِنْ فَوْقِ الْاَرْضِ مَا لَهَا مِنْ قَرَارٍ

See how Allah sets forth a parable. - A goodly word (La Ilaha Illallah) is like a goodly tree, whose root is firmly fixed, and its branches (reach) the sky. Giving its fruit at all times, by the permission of its Lord and Allah, sets forth parables for mankind so that they may remember. And the parable of an evil word is an evil tree uprooted from the earth's surface, having no stability. (Ibrahim:24-26)

مَثَلُ الَّذِيْنَ اتَّخَذُوْا مِنْ دُوْنِ اللهِ اَوْلِيَآءَ كَمَثَلِ الْعَنْكَبُوْتِ ۖ اِتَّخَذَتْ بَيْتًا ۗ وَ اِنَّ اَوْهَنَ الْبُيُوْتِ لَبَيْتُ الْعَنْكَبُوْتِ ۘ لَوْ كَانُوْا يَعْلَمُوْنَ

The parable of those who take protectors (helpers) other than Allah is as the likeness of a spider, who builds (for itself) a house, but verily, the frailest (weakest) of houses is the spider's house; if they but knew. (Ankabut:41)

The Royal "We"

- In Arabic, this type of "We" is called the 'plural of someone who is exalting himself' – it is considered suitable for God, but for human beings it is a sign of arrogance.
- This is not a plural form for more than one God, as some critics of the Quran claim.
- In English, this is similar to the linguistic structure known as the "royal 'we'".
- Allah uses the plural form "We" to show His Power and Majesty.
- The verses below demonstrate the appropriate use of 'We' to show that Allah is in control.

إِنَّا فَتَحْنَا لَكَ فَتْحًا مُّبِينًا

Verily, **We** have given you a clear victory. (Surah Fath:1)

إِنَّا نَحْنُ نَزَّلْنَا الذِّكْرَ وَ إِنَّا لَهُ لَحْفِظُونَ

Verily, **We** have sent down this Dhikr (i.e., the Quran) (Surah Al Hijr:9)

إِنَّا أَنْزَلْنَهُ فِي لَيْلَةِ الْقَدْرِ

Verily, **We** have revealed it (the Quran) in the Night of Power (Surah Al Qadr: 1)

Details of the unseen world and our approach towards them

- There are two types of verses in the Quran: Muhkam and Mutashabihaat.
- The latter are verses that mention things beyond human knowledge and observation, or pertain to matters of the Hereafter or the unseen world.
- Such things are said in the form of comparison (tashbih) to something that we are aware of in our language and through our own experience in this world.
- The meaning of these verses is obvious, but their reality is unknown.

The description of Paradise that the pious have been promised is that in it are rivers of water, the taste and smell of which are not changed; rivers of milk of which the taste never changes; rivers of wine delicious to those who drink; and rivers of clarified honey (clear and pure) therein for them is every kind of fruit; and forgiveness from their Lord. (Muhammad:15)

عَلَيْهَا تِسْعَةَ عَشَرَ

It (hell) has nineteen (angels) guardians (Mudhatthir:30)

- The Quran's argument is simple. If we have no source of knowledge other than Allah and His Prophets about matters that cannot be seen, observed, or comprehended, what is the point of going after them? Their meanings are clear, but their actual reality is unknown.
- For example, when the Quran states that there will be nineteen guardian angels in Hell, we should not inquire, 'Why nineteen?' Why does Hell require guardians? How big will the guardians be? Will nineteen be enough?

وَ الَّذِيۡ اَنۡزَلَ عَلَیۡکَ الۡکِتٰبَ مِنۡہُ اٰیٰتٌ مُّحۡکَمٰتٌ ہُنَّ اُمُّ الۡکِتٰبِ وَ اُخَرُ مُتَشٰبِہٰتٌ ۚ فَاَمَّا الَّذِیۡنَ فِیۡ قُلُوۡبِہِمۡ زَیۡغٌ فَیَتَّبِعُوۡنَ مَا تَشَابَہَ مِنۡہُ ابۡتِغَآءَ الۡفِتۡنَةِ وَ ابۡتِغَآءَ تَاۡوِیۡلِہٖ ۚ صّ ۚ وَ مَا یَعۡلَمُ تَاۡوِیۡلَہٗۤ اِلَّا اللّٰهُ ۟ وَ الرّٰسِخُوۡنَ فِی الۡعِلۡمِ یَقُوۡلُوۡنَ اٰمَنَّا بِہٖ ۙ کُلٌّ مِّنۡ عِنۡدِ رَبِّنَا

He has revealed this Book with verses that are *Muhkam* also – they are the foundation of the Book – and some others [besides them] that are *Mutashabihaat*. Then those whose hearts are perverted always go after the *Mutashabihaat* from among it to create dissension and to know their reality, even though no one except God knows their reality. On the other hand, those who are well-grounded in this knowledge say: "We believe in them: all this is from our Lord."

Parallel Verses and Explanation

- The Quran presents its message in various ways and styles.
- The same subject or story is repeated at multiple places with different details, and is relevant to the context in which it comes.
- In the Quran, there is no meaningless repetition.
- The Quran is unique in that its verses often explain other verses.
- Scholars of the Quran agree that to understand its verses, it is best to refer to the Quran itself first.
- At one place, an aspect would be hidden, while at another, it would be exposed.
- The initially revealed verses were concise, brief, and succinct, and later verses explained them.

وَ لَقَدْ صَرَّفْنَا فِي هٰذَا الْقُرْاٰنِ لِيَذَّكَّرُوْا

الَّرٰ كِتٰبٌ أُحْكِمَتْ اٰيٰتُهٗ ثُمَّ فُصِّلَتْ مِنْ لَّدُنْ حَكِيمٍ خَبِيرٍ

"And we have explained in various ways Our revelations in this Quran so that they may take heed." (Bani Israel:41)

This is a Book whose verses were first concise, then explained by Him, who is wise and all-knowing. (Hud:1)

اَللّٰهُ نَزَّلَ اَحْسَنَ الْحَدِيْثِ كِتٰبًا مُّتَشَابِهًا مَّثَانِيَ

[O People!] God has revealed the best of discourses in the form of a Book whose verses resemble one another and whose Surahs occur in pairs (Zumr:23)

Conclusion

While maintaining the simplicity and flow of the prose and the rhythm of poetry, the Quran provides sound reasoning for its arguments, subtly harmonizes and connects topics, shifts its stresses, cites stories and anecdotes, and swings back and forth from its central theme, intimidates, encourages, and emotionally attaches with its readers in a unique way.

Discussion and Assignment

Why are some of the stories in the Quran repeated many times?

Can I sing the Quran with musical instruments?

Read a story in the Quran that has a dialogue between two characters of the Quran, ready to present the next lesson

Chapter 5

Characters in the Quran

In this chapter, we will discuss the various characters the Quran addresses directly or indirectly.

Characters in the Quran

Prophets	Believers	Hypocrites	Gabriel	Angels

Polytheists	Satan	People of the Book

- A structured conversation between the above characters of 7th-century Arabia can be observed in the words of God in the Quran. It either originates from God or from one of them and is directed to one or more of them. These characters speak to each other, and the conversation rapidly shifts back and forth between them.

يَا أَيُّهَا الَّذِينَ آمَنُوا كُلُوا مِنْ طَيِّبَاتِ مَا رَزَقْنَاكُمْ

O you who believe! Eat of the lawful things that We have provided you with (Baqarah:172).

يَا أَيُّهَا النَّبِيُّ إِنَّا أَرْسَلْنَاكَ شَاهِدًا وَمُبَشِّرًا وَنَذِيرًا

O Prophet, verily, We have sent you as a witness, and a bearer of glad tidings, and a warner (Ahzab:45)

إِذَا جَاءَكَ الْمُنَافِقُونَ قَالُوا نَشْهَدُ إِنَّكَ لَرَسُولُ اللَّهِ

When the hypocrites come to you, [O Muhammad], they say, "We testify that you are the Messenger of Allah." (Munafiqoon:71)

يَا أَهْلَ الْكِتَابِ لِمَ تَلْبِسُونَ الْحَقَّ بِالْبَاطِلِ

O People of the Book: "Why do you conceal truth with falsehood (Aal-e-Imran:71)

إِنَّ الشَّيْطَانَ لِلْإِنْسَانِ عَدُوٌّ مُبِينٌ

Indeed, Satan is an open enemy of man (Yusuf:5)

نَزَلَ بِهِ الرُّوحُ الْأَمِينُ

Which is brought down by the Rooh Al Ameen (Gabriel) (Shuara:193)

وَ إِنْ أَحَدٌ مِّنَ الْمُشْرِكِينَ اسْتَجَارَكَ فَأَجِرْهُ حَتَّى يَسْمَعَ كَلَمَ اللهِ

And if anyone of the Mushrikun seeks your protection, then grant him protection, so that he may hear the Word of Allah (the Quran) (Tawbah:06)

Shift of the Speaker and the Addressee

- As noticed in the previous examples, the characters in the Quran speak to one another, and the conversation shifts rapidly among them. If these "leaps" of conversation are accounted for, much of the apparent disjointedness of the discourse can become meaningful as a well-directed dialogue between the characters.
- The discourse/sermon is sometimes directed towards a specific addressee, sometimes towards multiple addressees, and at other times it is a monologue that does not directly address anyone.
- Sometimes, people are addressed indirectly – the message is not directed toward the apparent addressee.
- There are instances when what is said is actually not uttered, but said in the heart.
- The shift expresses emotions ranging from love to hate, from rebuke to praise.
- Sometimes, what is understood to be implied is left out and not said in words.
- These shifts in utterances and emotions stir the mind and stimulate the soul, and must be appreciated to have a deeper understanding of the Quran.

Verses starting from "Qul"

تِلْكَ أَمَانِيُّهُمْ قُلْ هَاتُوا بُرْهَانَكُمْ إِنْ كُنْتُمْ صَادِقِينَ

That is [merely] their wishful thinking. Say (O Muhammad), "Bring your proof, if you are truthful." (Baqarah:111)

قُلْ هُوَ اللهُ أَحَدٌ

State clearly (announce) that Allah is unique and one (Ikhlaas:1)

- The word "Qul" (generally translated as "Say") is used hundreds of times in the Quran – sometimes at the beginning of the verse and sometimes in the middle of the verse.
- Since the Quran is conveyed through the Prophet, it can be said that the command "Say" implicitly precedes every verse; however, in some verses, it is explicitly stated.
- The nature of the word "Say" is different in different verses:
  - Support an authoritative declaration from God.
  - When God chooses not to address certain individuals due to their behavior.
  - Answering a question (ask them).
  - Announcing and declaring something.
  - Sometimes, it appears in the singular but actually directs believers to respond (more than once).
  - Making a decisive statement in the end as a result of a long debate or argument.

Key considerations when understanding the Quran

1 The Quran is a speech of God compiled in 114 Surahs. Of these speeches, the addressees of each surah and its verses must be determined from among the people present at the time of the revelation of the Quran.

2 Depending on the primary and secondary addressees of the surah and its verses, the preceding pronoun, the referred-to entity of every definite article (alif lam), and the connotation of every term and expression must be connected back to its intended addressees.

3 Each surah's ambiance must be carefully examined – situation, background, and requisites. It should be determined from within the surah and not from outside. The verses may contain issues related to the local and prevalent culture of that time.

4 The direction of its address shifts very quickly - multiple times in Surah and sometimes even within a verse. When delivering direct statements, the speaker may also shift very quickly. The orator shifts from one addressee to another, switching his tone, expressions, and the grandeur of his words. These shifts must be noted carefully. Otherwise, it will appear as disjointed text.

5 General and specific verses should be differentiated. Generic verses are the verses that are not limited to time, place and person.

6 For example, in the case of directives given concerning the punishment associated with messengers, the supremacy of political authority, and the supremacy of the true religion of God, it must be determined carefully if the directives are permanent or related explicitly to the addressees of the prophet's time and cannot be extended beyond that

7 Only those nations, stories, places, and other aspects come in the Quran which are known to its direct addressees. It is an ineffective way of giving the message when a reference is given that the audience is completely unaware of

Discussion and Assignment

If there are so many subtle shifts in the text of the Quran, then how can we say that the Quran delivers its message with clarity?

Why is it important to identify the addressee of the verse?

Why does the Quran not mention or address Buddhists or Hindus?

Read at least 10 verses of the Quran of your choice and decide who the addressee is from the text

Chapter 6

Theme / Topic of the Quran

In this chapter, we will discuss the Quran's central theme and how its topics relate to it.

Topics and Themes – Example

- Read this passage carefully. This is taken from a book that is written for teenagers.

You already have the key to unlocking your real personality and fearlessly creating your authentic life free of labels and comparisons – you just need to be shown how.

Labels and comparisons stop you from being your real self.

You try to live up to an ideal - to be like the teen you think is smarter, better looking, and more popular than you…

And when you do that - when you try to be something you're not - you're living under false pretenses.

This is when the domino effect kicks in: you start to live in fear that someone may find out who you *really* are. It wrecks your self-esteem, personal power, and any belief that you deserve much more.

That's a lonely place to be and no way to live your life, right?

But it doesn't have to be that way.

Whether you're a nerd or a jock, an overachiever or an underachiever, a loner or an outcast - that is not your entire identity. It's just one tiny part of the vast YOU.

With the help of this book, you can **uncover the whole, wonderful person within** and, from that, create an incredible life on your own terms.

Here are just a few of the things that you will discover inside:

- **5 simple steps to find your uniqueness and embrace the amazing personality you didn't know you had**
- How you can get rid of the negative beliefs about yourself and get your self-confidence back
- **4 things you can do to escape the comparative trap and live from your authentic self**
- How to be the "ruler of your kingdom" and keep the people you want inside your castle walls…and the others out
- How following the example of *The Three Musketeers* will manifest in miraculous ways in your life
- **6 effective ways to stop a bully in their tracks**
- 7 celebrities who overcame all odds and dominated through their individuality
- **The "1 in 60" rule that will change the way you think about failure**

- Can you guess the theme of the book from which this passage is taken?
- What is the topic of this passage?
- What does this sentence mean in this passage: "*How to be the ruler of your kingdom and keep the people you want inside your castle walls.*"
- How is the theme and topic affecting the meaning of the above statement?

God's Scheme for this World

- The religious history of mankind can be divided into the Prophetic Era (the major portion) and the Post-Prophetic Era (we are living)

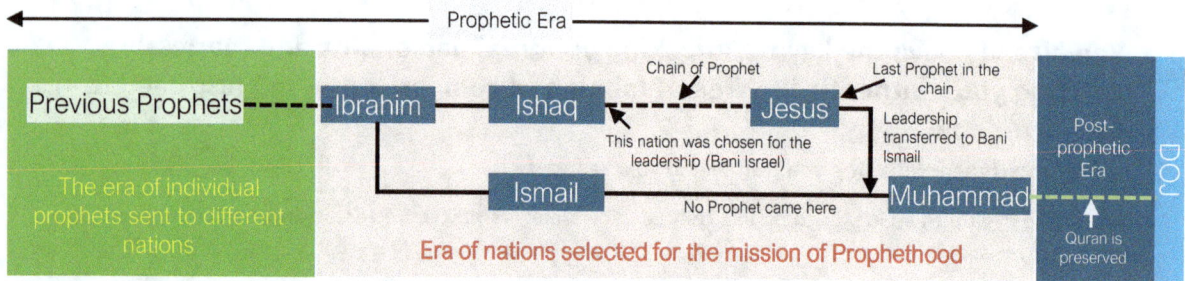

- Within the Prophetic Era, there are two distinct phases:
  - The era of individual prophets sent to different nations.
  - The era of nations selected as leaders to carry God's message.
- Within the Prophetic Era, there is a practice of God in which when He sends a Messenger (Rasool) among a nation, He punishes them in this world if they reject the Messenger, and saves the Messenger and his followers from that nation.
- The divine punishment comes in two forms: natural disasters and Messengers. His companions punish the rejectors through war, killing them in battle.
- This practice of Allah (called *Sunnatullah*) is eternally preserved in the Quran to remain with us in the Post-Prophetic Era.
- This practice is not related to the eternal Shariah of God and is only specific to the people, time, and place.
- This practice of divine punishment ended after Prophet Muhammad.

وَ لِكُلِّ أُمَّةٍ رَّسُوۡلٌ فَاِذَا جَآءَ رَسُوۡلُهُمۡ قُضِیَ بَیۡنَهُمۡ بِالۡقِسۡطِ وَ هُمۡ لَا یُظۡلَمُوۡنَ

For each community, there is a messenger. Then, when their messenger comes, their fate is decided (in this world) fairly, and no injustice is shown to them. (Yunus:47)

سُنَّةَ مَنۡ قَدۡ اَرۡسَلۡنَا قَبۡلَکَ مِنۡ رُّسُلِنَا وَ لَا تَجِدُ لِسُنَّتِنَا تَحۡوِیۡلًا

Bear in mind the practice about the messengers We had sent before you, and you will not find any change in Our practice (about the consequences they faced for rejecting the messenger). (Bani Israel:77)

رُسُلًا مُّبَشِّرِیۡنَ وَ مُنۡذِرِیۡنَ لِئَلَّا یَکُوۡنَ لِلنَّاسِ عَلَی اللّٰهِ حُجَّةٌۢ بَعۡدَ الرُّسُلِ وَ کَانَ اللّٰهُ عَزِیۡزًا حَکِیۡمًا

These messengers were sent as bearers of glad tidings and warnings so that after them, people are left with no excuse that they can present before God. (Nisaa:165)

God's law of conclusive communication of the Truth

- This important law that is quite visible from the Quran is summarized below:

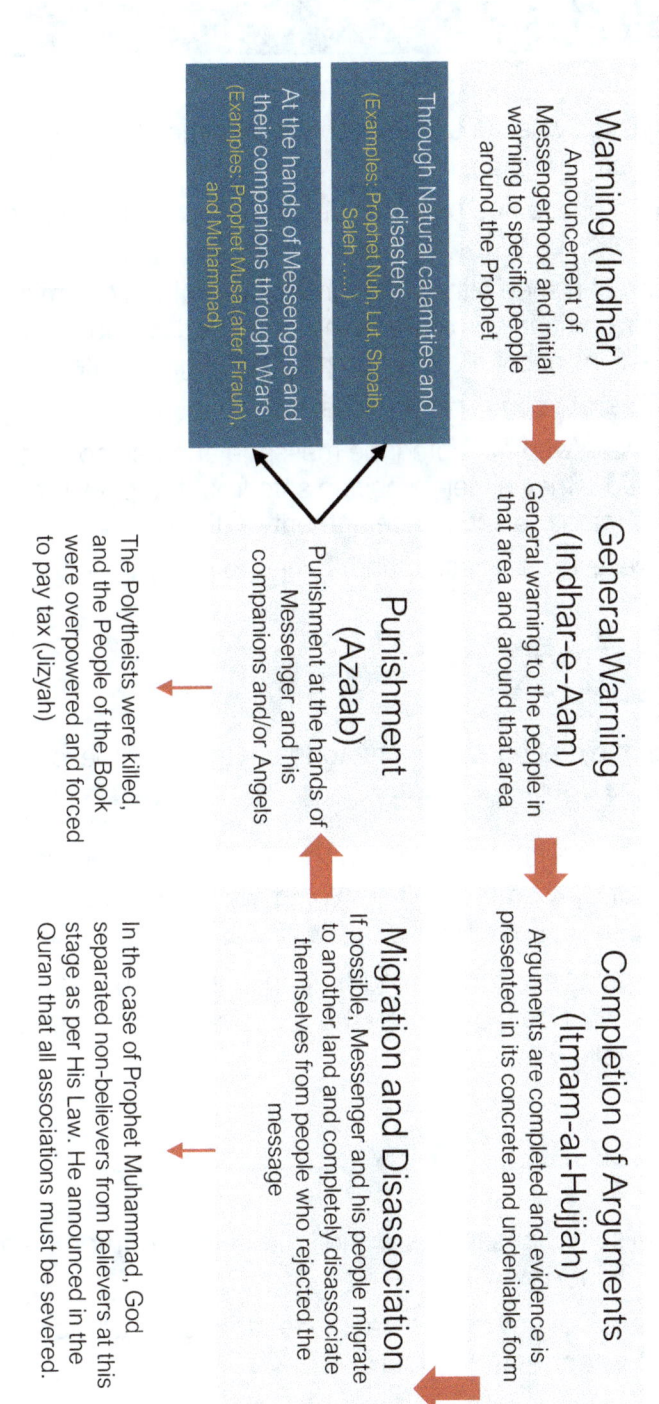

This law defines different phases in Prophet Muhammad's mission and must be taken into consideration when understanding the Quran

Warning (Indhar)
Announcement of Messengerhood and initial warning to specific people around the Prophet

General Warning (Indhar-e-Aam)
General warning to the people in that area and around that area

Completion of Arguments (Itmam-al-Hujjah)
Arguments are completed and evidence is presented in its concrete and undeniable form

Migration and Disassociation
If possible, Messenger and his people migrate to another land and completely disassociate themselves from people who rejected the message

Punishment (Azaab)
Punishment at the hands of Messenger and his companions and/or Angels

Through Natural calamities and disasters
(Examples: Prophet Nuh, Lut, Shoaib, Saleh .....)

At the hands of Messengers and their companions through Wars
(Examples: Prophet Musa (after Firaun), and Muhammad)

The Polytheists were killed, and the People of the Book were overpowered and forced to pay tax (Jizyah)

In the case of Prophet Muhammad, God separated non-believers from believers at this stage as per His Law. He announced in the Quran that all associations must be severed.

God's law of conclusive communication of the Truth

The Quran's central theme is the documentation of the account of Prophet Muhammad's warning mission (*Indhar*) to his people and the people around him that happened according to the Law of Conclusive Communication of the Truth

- The divine court of justice was set up for the nations of the Messengers in this world after the phase of Itmam al Hujjah.
- By the Itmam al Hujjah phase, the believers become distinct and separated from the disbelievers.
- The disbelievers were punished either through various natural calamities if the Messenger had fewer companions or through wars (killed or subjugated) if there were enough companions and if there was a place to migrate safely.
- It was due to the deliberate denial of the disbelievers.
- On the other hand, those who accepted the message and helped Messenger in his mission were rewarded – they either remained safe from the punishment or were given power over the rejectors and hence authority in the land.
- In this process, the believers are tested and trained to purify their hearts and their belief in God.

فَلَمَّا جَآءَهُم مَّا عَرَفُوا كَفَرُوا بِهِ ۚ فَلَعْنَةُ اللهِ عَلَى الْكَٰفِرِينَ

So, when that which they recognized came to them, they disbelieved in it. So let the curse of Allah be on the disbelievers. (2:89)

- The punishment and humiliation inflicted upon the Messenger's nation was God's retribution carried out by God Himself, in which the Messenger and his companions were nothing but divine weapons.
- The purpose of this practice is to remind humanity about the Day of Judgment and the accountability on that day, based on the knowledge that we have been given and the actions that follow that knowledge.

- Why does Allah punish nations in this world when every human being will be judged on the Day of Judgment?
- What is the significance of saving the entire life story and struggle of Prophet Muhammad as a Messenger in the Quran?

Quran talks about the phases
Examples

General Warning

يَا أَيُّهَا الْمُدَّثِّرُ ۚ قُمْ فَأَنذِرْ

O, you enwrapped in the shawl! Arise and heighten the warning. (74:1-2)

Disassociation and Migration

قُلْ يَا أَيُّهَا الْكَافِرُونَ ۚ لَا أَعْبُدُ مَا تَعْبُدُونَ ۚ وَ لَا أَنتُمْ عَابِدُونَ مَا أَعْبُدُ

وَ لَا أَنَا عَابِدٌ مَّا عَبَدتُّمْ ۚ وَ لَا أَنتُمْ عَابِدُونَ مَا أَعْبُدُ

لَكُمْ دِينُكُمْ وَلِيَ دِينِ

Declare you [O Prophet!]: "O Disbelievers! I shall not worship those you worship. And you will never worship [alone] He whom I worship. And [before this] never was I prepared to worship those you have worshipped. And neither were you ever prepared to worship [alone] whom I have been worshipping. [So, now] to you, your religion, and mine. (109)

The nations of Aad, Thamud, Noah, Lot, and Shoaib were destroyed

فَكُلًّا أَخَذْنَا بِذَنبِهِ ۚ فَمِنْهُم مَّنْ أَرْسَلْنَا عَلَيْهِ حَاصِبًا وَمِنْهُم مَّنْ أَخَذَتْهُ الصَّيْحَةُ وَمِنْهُم مَّنْ خَسَفْنَا بِهِ الْأَرْضَ وَمِنْهُم مَّنْ أَغْرَقْنَا ۚ وَمَا كَانَ اللَّهُ لِيَظْلِمَهُمْ وَلَٰكِن كَانُوا أَنفُسَهُمْ يَظْلِمُونَ ۝

So, each of them We seized for their crime: of them, against some, We sent a violent tornado with showers of stones; a mighty blast caught some; some We had sunk in the earth, and some We drowned in the waters. (29:40)

The people of Prophet Muhammad (Polytheists) were killed with swords

قَاتِلُوهُمْ يُعَذِّبْهُمُ اللهُ بِأَيْدِيكُمْ وَ يُخْزِهِمْ وَ يَنصُرْكُمْ عَلَيْهِمْ وَ يَشْفِ صُدُورَ قَوْمٍ مُّؤْمِنِينَ

Fight with them, and God will punish them with your hands, humiliate them, and help you to victory over them, and bring comfort to the hearts of a group of believers. (Tawbah:14)

Punishment phase in the Quran

The people of Prophet Muhammad (Polytheists) were killed with swords

فَلَمْ تَقْتُلُوهُمْ وَ لَكِنَّ اللهَ قَتَلَهُمْ

[Believers!] It is not you who killed them; it was, in fact, God who killed them. (Anfal:17)

The People of the Book, from among the nation of Prophet Muhammad and the nations around him, were subjugated

قَاتِلُوا الَّذِينَ لَا يُؤْمِنُوْنَ بِاللهِ وَ لَا بِالْيَوْمِ الْآخِرِ وَ لَا يُحَرِّمُوْنَ مَا حَرَّمَ اللهُ وَ رَسُوْلُهُ وَ لَا يَدِيْنُوْنَ دِيْنَ الْحَقِّ مِنَ الَّذِيْنَ أُوْتُوا الْكِتٰبَ حَتّٰى يُعْطُوا الْجِزْيَةَ عَنْ يَّدٍ وَّ هُمْ صٰغِرُوْنَ

Fight with those who believe not in Allah, nor in the Last Day, nor forbid that which has been forbidden by Allah and His Messenger, and those who acknowledge not the religion of truth (i.e., Islam) among the people of the Scripture (Jews and Christians), until they pay the Jizyah with willing submission, and feel subdued. (Tawbah:29)

Key considerations when understanding the Quran

- **General verses** (applicable to all times, places, and people) and **specific verses** (applicable to specific times, places, and people) should be differentiated.
- For example, in the case of Jihad directives given about the punishment associated with messengers, the supremacy of political authority, and the supremacy of the true religion of God, it must be clearly understood that these directives were specifically related to the addressees of the Prophet's time and cannot be extended beyond that.
- For example, God commanded the believers not to take Jews and Christians as their friends after the phase of Itmam al Hujjah is over – this directive cannot be extended to today's Jews and Christians.
- For example, today, people cannot be called Kaafir or Rejectors because we have no way to do the Itmam al Hujjah the way the Prophet did in the guidance of God – A Kaafir is a person who has understood the message properly and considers it true after it has been given in the clearest manner possible but still rejects it for any reason (arrogance, bias, social pressure, group association, etc.).
- For example, today, the state cannot kill someone who has changed his religion and left Islam.

Chapter 7

Arrangement of the Quran

In this chapter, we will discuss the arrangement of the chapters in the Quran as we see it now and how this arrangement relates to the Quran's central theme.

Order of revelation vs order of compilation

Order of Revelation
Surahs revealed according to the situation and demand

is NOT THE SAME as

Order of Compilation
The order in which Surahs are written today

The Quran is revealed in piecemeal

- The Quran has been revealed piecemeal according to the time and circumstances of the Prophet's mission.
- The Prophet received guidance in the form of verses when needed, although he sometimes wished to have it all at once.
- The order in which it was arranged for recitation (as we have it today) was different from the order in which it was revealed (the chronological order).
- The Prophet instructed the scribes of the Quran to write the revealed verses in the new order, where they should be, and the Prophet and his companions also memorized the Quran in that order.
- Once its initial revelation was over, the archangel Gabriel read it to the Prophet multiple times in the new order. Also, in this final recital, temporary directives were either revised or permanently deleted.
- The Quran, in its new version, was compiled during the lifetime of the Prophet.
- This is just one of the orders of revelation reported by historians. Some other historians have reported a different order. Knowing this order is not required to understand the Quran.

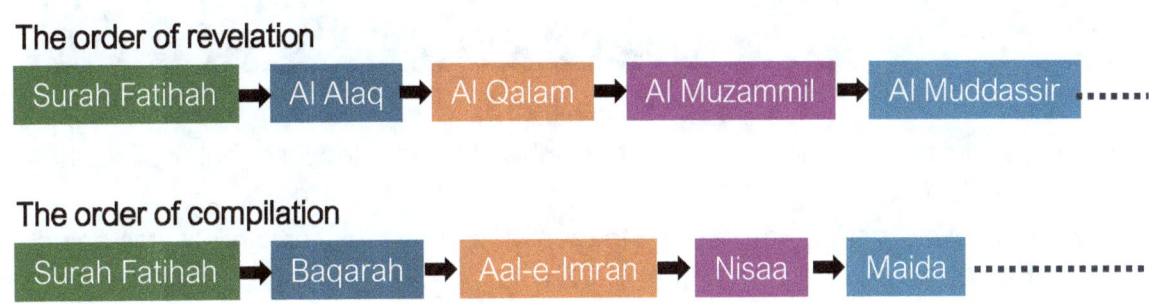

The order of revelation

Surah Fatihah → Al Alaq → Al Qalam → Al Muzammil → Al Muddassir ......

The order of compilation

Surah Fatihah → Baqarah → Aal-e-Imran → Nisaa → Maida ....

The Quran records its own plan

وَ قَالَ الَّذِیْنَ كَفَرُوْا لَوْ لَا نُزِّلَ عَلَیْهِ الْقُرْاٰنُ جُمْلَةً وَّاحِدَةً ۛ كَذٰلِكَ ۛ لِنُثَبِّتَ بِهٖ فُؤَادَكَ وَ رَتَّلْنٰهُ تَرْتِیْلًا

The disbelievers said, "Why is the Quran not revealed to him all at once?" This is how we reveal that we can gradually strengthen your heart in stages. (Furqan:32)

لَا تُحَرِّكْ بِهٖ لِسَانَكَ لِتَعْجَلَ بِهٖ ۙ   اِنَّ عَلَیْنَا جَمْعَهٗ وَ قُرْاٰنَهٗ ۚ

فَاِذَا قَرَاْنٰهُ فَاتَّبِعْ قُرْاٰنَهٗ ۚ   ثُمَّ اِنَّ عَلَیْنَا بَیَانَهٗ ؕ

Don't move your tongue in haste to get it all (O Muhammad), its collection and recitation (final recitation) is upon Us, and when we have recited it to you, follow its recitation. Then its explanation is upon Us (Qiyamah:16-19)

> Narrated Qatadah: I asked Anas Ibn Malik: 'Who collected (compiled) the Quran at the time of the Prophet?' He replied: 'Four, all of whom were from the Ansar: Ubay Ibn Kaab, Muadh Ibn Jabal, Zayd Ibn Thabit, and Abu Zayd.'(Bukhari, Book 61, #525))

- When Gabriel brought this Surah to the Prophet, he repeated it so that the Prophet could memorize it firmly.
- The Prophet was instructed not to try to memorize the revelation while it was being given. Rather, he should listen to it attentively.
- God will ensure that he fully commits it to his memory and can recite it accurately. He is also assured that he will neither forget a word of it nor make any mistake in reciting it.
- God gave His complete plan: once the complete revelation is over, He will collect the Quran as a whole, recite it to him through the Angel Gabriel as it should be recited by all Muslims, and explain anything that requires explanation.

Makki vs Madani Surah

- The portion of the Quran that was revealed in Makkah is called Makki, and the portion of the Quran that was revealed in Medinah is called Madani.
- The majority of the Quran (some say 2/3rd) was revealed in Makkah.

	Makki	Madani
Main addressees	Quraish, Polytheists, Muslims	People of the Book, Muslims as a new nation, Hypocrites, Polytheists
Main Subjects	Monotheism, evidence of monotheism, rejection of polytheism, belief in Allah, DOJ, Prophethood, Books, Angels, and Fate	Test and trials for the believers, instructions for the Muslims as a nation, Final warning and punishment for disbelievers
Law	Basic human morals and character is discussed and encouraged with no law given	The Shariah is revealed for the Muslims in their individual and collective capacity
Stories	The stories of Messengers and Prophets and their destruction in this world if they rejected their Messengers	Few stories and what is about to happen with the nation of the Prophet
Length	Short Surahs	Long Surahs

Six (6) Main Phases of Prophetic Mission

- Remember, we described these 6 major phases in the lifetime of a Messenger that demonstrate the Day of Judgment on a smaller scale.
- The description of that small-scale Day of Judgement that happened in Arabia as a result of Prophet Muhammad's Itmam al Hujjah has been eternally preserved in the Quran in this subtle sequence of phases.

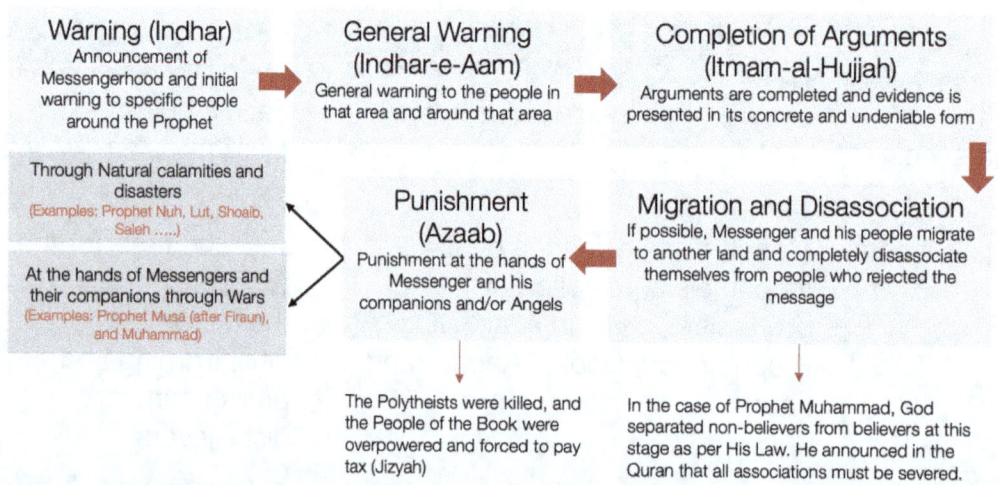

Phase	Topic	Period	Explanation
0	Commissioning	Makkah	Prophet is commissioned
1	Warning (Indhar)	Makkah	Warning to people in the close circle
2	Enhanced Warning (Indhar e Aam)	Makkah	Public Warning to everyone around
3	Conclusive Arguments (Itmam al Hujjah)	Makkah	Presenting the final arguments
4	Migration & Acquittal (Hijrah wa Bara'ah)	Makkah	Leaving the place and cutting ties
5	Purification and Practices of Muslims	Madinah	Preparing Muslims for battles and reward
6	Reward and Punishment	Madinah	Final verdict given for each group

- Phase 0 is the commissioning phase, which happens in the form of an event or two, and the Prophet is informed that he has been assigned a responsibility.
- The Warning phase is the first phase of the complete mission.

Context and Coherence in the Quran

- Context and coherence play a crucial role in the arrangement of the Quran, both at the level of the Surah and at a higher level.
- Each Surah of the Quran is a coherent whole, a complete unit, and has a theme.
- The verses within a Surah, Surahs within a Chapter, and Chapters within the Quran are arranged in a specific sequence that is divinely ordained according to the theme of the unit (Surah, Chapter, or the Quran).
- The topics progress in an orderly fashion, with each new sub-topic emerging from the previous one.
- The context in which the verse appears is crucial in determining the correct meaning of the words that appear in the verse.
- **This coherence ensures that there is only one meaning of the verse, word, or message given in the Quran.**
- This coherence is the door through which the real wisdom of the Quran can be reached, and the conflicts can be avoided within the collective body of Muslims. The Quran directs us to turn to it to resolve all differences in religious matters.

القران لا يحتمل الا تاويلا واحدا

There is no possibility of more than one interpretation of the Quran. (Imam Hamid Uddin Farahi)

- In the absence of appreciating the coherence in the Quran, people will have a different opinion about the meaning that a verse or a word is trying to deliver.
- If the context and coherence in this divine arrangement are taken into consideration, then it reduces the chances of interpreting a verse in multiple ways to almost none.

وَإِنْ كُنتُمْ فِي رَيْبٍ مِمَّا نَزَّلْنَا عَلَى عَبْدِنَا فَأْتُوا بِسُورَةٍ مِنْ مِثْلِهِ وَادْعُوا شُهَدَاءَكُمْ مِنْ دُونِ اللَّهِ إِنْ كُنتُمْ صَادِقِينَ

And if you doubt what We have revealed to Our servant, then [go and] produce **a single** Surah like it. And [for this purpose] also call your leaders besides Allah if you are truthful [in your claim]. (Baqarah:23)

أَمْ يَقُولُونَ افْتَرَاهُ قُلْ فَأْتُوا بِعَشْرِ سُوَرٍ مِثْلِهِ مُفْتَرَيَاتٍ وَ ادْعُوا مَنِ اسْتَطَعْتُمْ مِّن دُونِ اللهِ إِن كُنْتُمْ صِدِقِينَ

Do they say: "The Prophet has fabricated it himself?" [134] Tell them: Then you also bring forth **ten (10)** such fabricated surahs like it and call in whoever you can except God, if you are truthful. (Hud:13)

Coherence Examples

Example 1

وَ قَالُوا لَوْ لَا نُزِّلَ عَلَيْهِ اٰيَةٌ مِّنْ رَّبِّهٖ ۚ قُلْ اِنَّ اللهَ قَادِرٌ عَلٰٓى اَنْ يُّنَزِّلَ اٰيَةً وَّ لٰكِنَّ اَكْثَرَ هُمْ لَا يَعْلَمُوْنَ

وَ مَا مِنْ دَآبَّةٍ فِي الْاَرْضِ وَ لَا طٰٓئِرٍ يَّطِيْرُ بِجَنَاحَيْهِ اِلَّآ اُمَمٌ اَمْثَالُكُمْ ۚ مَا فَرَّطْنَا فِي الْكِتٰبِ مِنْ شَيْءٍ ۚ ثُمَّ اِلٰى

رَبِّهِمْ يُحْشَرُوْنَ ۞ وَ الَّذِيْنَ كَذَّبُوْا بِاٰيٰتِنَا صُمٌّ وَّ بُكْمٌ فِي الظُّلُمٰتِ ۗ مَنْ يَّشَإِ اللهُ يُضْلِلْهُ ۚ

وَ مَنْ يَّشَأْ يَجْعَلْهُ عَلٰى صِرَاطٍ مُّسْتَقِيْمٍ

And they said: "Why is no sign sent down to him from his Lord?" Say: "Allah is certainly able to send down a sign, but most of them are not aware of its reality." (Don't you see) There is no moving creature on earth, nor a bird that flies with its two wings, but communities are like you. (When it comes to signs) We have not neglected much in the Book, then (what is left now) that they (all) shall be gathered in front of God. Those who reject Our Signs (proofs, evidence) are deaf and dumb in darkness. Allah sends astray whom He wills, and He guides on the Straight Path whom He wills. (Anaam:37-39)

- If the section of the verse (in a different color) is read in isolation, then it would mean, "We did not leave anything out of this Book."

- The context of the verse is that the disbelievers would demand a sign to profess faith – it is evident from the next verse (verse 40) that the sign here refers to the punishment they are threatened with.

- The Quran argues that they do not fathom the implications of the sign of punishment because, after that, there is no respite.

- God told them that instead of asking for that Sign to believe, they should look around and find many signs in God's creation, such as the communities of animals and birds.

- When it comes to the evidence around us of a Powerful and Wise God, there is plenty, and nothing has been left out of it.

Example 2

There is no doubt that this is an honorable Quran in a protected Book (*Lauh al Mahfooz*). None but the purified (angels) have touched it, a revelation from the Lord of the Worlds (Waqiah:77-80)

- If the section of the verse (in a different color) is read in isolation, then it has been translated as, "none can touch it except the purified ones (for example, ones with Wudu) – which has become the source of a ruling in Islam that a person should not touch the Quran without Wudu.

- The context in which this verse has come is this:
    - The disbelievers have hurled an allegation against the Quran that this Quran was brought or taught to the Prophet by the Satan Jinns (due to the unique nature of the Book).
    - The Quran responds to such allegations, stating that this Book is from God Almighty and is preserved in a protected Book (in God's care). No one, except pure angels (Archangel Jibrael), has touched it, and only Jibrael delivers it to the Prophet.

- In this context, it is quite clear that this verse has nothing to do with ablution – it is recommended to perform Wudu before reciting the Quran, but it is not mandatory.

Example 3 – No Coherence

- Let's look at this example, where we will first translate it the way most translators do, without keeping coherence in mind.

Translation	Topic	Verse
By the Fig and Olive	Fruits	وَ التِّينِ وَ الزَّيْتُونِ
And by Mount Sinai And by this peaceful city	Places	وَ طُورِ سِيْنِينَ وَ هٰذَا الْبَلَدِ الْاَمِيْنِ
We created human beings on the best of mold	Creation of human being	لَقَدْ خَلَقْنَا الْاِنْسَانَ فِيْ اَحْسَنِ تَقْوِيْمٍ
Then we threw him to the lowest of the low	Punishment	ثُمَّ رَدَدْنٰهُ اَسْفَلَ سٰفِلِيْنَ
Except for those who believed and did good, there is a reward for them	Reward for believers	اِلَّا الَّذِيْنَ اٰمَنُوْا وَ عَمِلُوا الصّٰلِحٰتِ فَلَهُمْ اَجْرٌ غَيْرُ مَمْنُوْنٍ
Now, what made you deny the retribution	Denying DOJ	فَمَا يُكَذِّبُكَ بَعْدُ بِالدِّيْنِ
Isn't Allah the best of the Judges	Praising Allah	اَلَيْسَ اللهُ بِاَحْكَمِ الْحٰكِمِيْنَ

- Does the flow of the verses make any sense? The Surah covers many topics, including fruit, cities, human beings, and their behavior.

Example 3 – With Coherence

- Let's look at this example and translate it with coherence in mind.

Translation	Verse
The Mount of Fig and Olive (birthplace of Jesus) bears witness	وَ التِّيْنِ وَ الزَّيْتُوْنِ
And by Mount Sinai (the place of Musa) And by this peaceful city (of Ibrahim) bear witness	وَ طُوْرِ سِيْنِيْنَ وَ هٰذَا الْبَلَدِ الْاَمِيْنِ
We raised the best human beings (nations) at these places	لَقَدْ خَلَقْنَا الْاِنْسَانَ فِيْ اَحْسَنِ تَقْوِيْمٍ
Then we reverted those to a low state who wanted to be low (punishment for rejection)	ثُمَّ رَدَدْنٰهُ اَسْفَلَ سٰفِلِيْنَ

Topic

The three best nations were raised at the time of their births. Only those who wanted to debase themselves were punished among those nations

Translation	Verse
Except for those who believed and did good, there is a reward for them	اِلَّا الَّذِيْنَ اٰمَنُوْا وَ عَمِلُوا الصّٰلِحٰتِ فَلَهُمْ اَجْرٌ غَيْرُ مَمْنُوْنٍ
Now, what made you deny the retribution	فَمَا يُكَذِّبُكَ بَعْدُ بِالدِّيْنِ
Isn't Allah the best of the Judges	اَلَيْسَ اللهُ بِاَحْكَمِ الْحٰكِمِيْنَ

Topic

Reward for believers among them
After seeing these results, would you still deny the DOJ

Understanding of Surah At-Tin in the light of the Phases

- The group of Surahs, Surah At-Tin (95) to Surah al-Quraysh (106), belongs to **Phase 3** of the mission, which is *Itmam al-Hujjah* (Conclusive Communication of the Truth).

- Surah At-Tin is at the beginning of that group. The theme of Surah al-Tin is to validate the Day of Judgment by providing examples from the past. It is substantiated conclusively; the Quraysh are reprimanded for their attitude towards it.

- It is evident from the details given above that the reward and punishment that will take place for all mankind on the Day of Judgement took place for the progeny of Ibrahim in this very world.

- The village of Fig, the mountains of Olive and Sinai, and the secure city of Makkah are all areas where reward and punishment manifested themselves with the people of three giant prophets, Isa, Musa, and Ibrahim. The Quran mentioned it in ascending order.

- When each branch of Ibrahim's progeny began, it was exactly in the best of states. It adhered to monotheism; had full conviction in the Hereafter, and its majority was of exemplary conduct.

- However, when it deviated from this status, God also relegated it to decadence, a condition evident for many centuries. It is afflicted with the scourge of humiliation and subjugation and is unable to find any way out of it.

Grouping of the Surahs

وَ لَقَدْ اٰتَيْنٰكَ سَبْعًا مِّنَ الْمَثَانِيْ وَ الْقُرْاٰنَ الْعَظِيْمَ

[O Prophet!] We have bestowed upon you seven pairs, which are the great Quran. (Hijr:87)

- The Quran comprises seven distinct groups/chapters (Abwaab), and within each chapter, Surahs occur in pairs, each addressing its respective theme.
- The Surahs in pairs complement each other in many ways if a deeper deliberation is done on every pair.
- Surah Al-Fatiha is an exception, as it introduces the entire Quran.
- Some Surahs, like Surah Nur and Ahzab, occur at the conclusion of the chapter without pairing with any other Surah. There are six unpaired Surahs.
- Each chapter of the Quran begins with one or more Makkan Surahs and ends with one or more Madinan Surahs.
- Within each chapter, the Surahs are in chronological order – the first Surah was revealed first.
- Each chapter discusses some aspect of the overall theme/topic of the Quran (the law of Itmam al Hujjah) by delineating some phase(s) of the warning.
- Each chapter has its own theme.

A different interpretation

- Some Mufassireen of the Quran suggest that this Ayah refers to Surah Fatiha. According to them, the translation of the verse is: "We have bestowed upon you seven oft-repeated verses and the Great Quran."
- The problems with this interpretation are:
  - Surah Fatiha has only six verses unless Bismillah is taken as the first verse of the Surah to make it seven. Others have divided the last verse into two, which cannot be the case. However, Bismillah is read before every Surah, so it cannot be a verse.
  - The correct and most appropriate translation of the word "*Mathani*" is "pairs" and is the plural of "*Mathna*," which means "pair," not oft repeated.
  - The verse refers to something that is either seven or equivalent to the Quran in subject matter.
  - "Wow" in the middle is the "wow" of explanation. The Quran comprises seven chapters, not Surah Fatiha.

Grouping of the Surahs

Chapter 1
Surah Fatiha (1) – Maidah (5)

Makkan: 1
Madinan: 2-5

Chapter 2
Surah Anaam (6) – Tawbah (9)

Makkan: 6-7
Madinan: 8-9

Chapter 3
Surah Yunus (10) – Nur (24)

Makkan: 10-23
Madinan: 24

Chapter 4
Surah Furqan (25) – Ahzab (33)

Makkan: 25-32
Madinan: 33

Chapter 5
Surah Saba (34) – Hujrat (49)

Makkan: 34-46
Madinan: 47-49

Chapter 6
Surah Qaaf (50) – Tahrim (66)

Makkan: 50-56
Madinan: 57-66

Chapter 7
Surah Mulk (67) – Naas (114)

Makkan: 67-112
Madinan: 113-114

Theme of the Groups

Group/Chapter 1

- Communicate the truth to the Jews and Christians to the extent that they are left with no excuse to deny it.
- Institute a new ummah from among the Ishmaelites.
- It's spiritual purification and isolation from the disbelievers.
- Description of its final covenant with God.

Group/Chapter 2

- Communicate the truth to the polytheists of Arabia to the extent that they are left with no excuse to deny it.
- Spiritual purification of the believers and their isolation from the disbelievers.
- A description of the final worldly Judgement of God.

Group/Chapter 3-6

- Delivering warning and glad tidings and spiritual purification of the believers.
- Their isolation from the disbelievers.

Group/Chapter 7

- Warn the leadership of the Quraysh of the consequences of the Hereafter.
- To communicate the truth to them to the extent that they are left with no excuse to deny it, and, as a result, to warn them of severe punishment.
- Give glad tidings to Prophet Muhammad for the dominance of his religion in the Arabian Peninsula.

The complete arrangement

Green: Makkan Surahs **Yellow:** Madinan Surahs. **Bold:** Unpaired Surahs
Not Bold: Paired Surahs   **Blue:** Chapters.   Red: Climax of the Quran

Chapter 1	**Fatihah (1),** Baqarah (2), Al-e-Imran (3), Nisa (4), Ma'idah (5)
Chapter 2	An'am (6), A'raf (7), Anfal (8), Tawbah (9)
Chapter 3	Yunus (10), Hud (11), Yusuf (12), Ra'd (13), Ibrahim (14), Hijr (15), Nahl (16), Bani Isra'il (17), Kahf (18), Maryam (19), Taha (20), Anbiya (21), Hajj (22), Mu'minun (23), **Nur (24)**
Chapter 4	Furqan (25), Shu'ara (26), Naml (27), Qasas (28), 'Ankabut (29), Rum (30), Luqman (31), Sajdah (32), **Ahzab (33)**
Chapter 5	Saba (34), Fatir (35), **Yasin (36),** Safaat (37), Su'ad (38), Zumar (39), Mu'min (40), Ham Mim Sajdah (41), Shurah (42), Zukhruf (43), Dukhan (44), Jathiyah (45), Muhammad (47), Fath (48), **Hujurat (49)**
Chapter 6	Qaf (50), Dhariyat (51), Tur (52), Najm (53), Qamar (54), Rahman (55), **Waq'iah (56),** Hadid (57), Mujadalah (58), Hashr (59), Mumtahinah (60), Saff (61), Jumu'ah (62), Munafiqun (63), Taghabun (64), Talaq (65), Tahrim (66)
Chapter 7	Mulk (67), Qalam (68), Haqqah (69), Ma'arij (70), Nuh (71), Jinn (72), Muzzammil (73), Muddaththir (74), Qiyamah (75), Dahr (76), Mursalat (77), Naba (78), Nazi'at (79), 'Abas (80), Takwir (81), Infitar (82), Mutaffifin (83), Inshiqaq (84), Buruj (85), Tariq (86), A'la (87), Ghashiyah (88), Fajr (89), Balad (90), Shams (91), Layl (92), Duha (93), Alam Nashrah (94), Tin (95), 'Alaq (96), Qadr (97), Bayyinah (98), Zilzal (99), 'Adiyat (100), Qari'ah (101), Takathur (102), 'Asr (103), Humazah (104), Fil (105), Quraysh (106), Ma'un (107), Kawthar (108), Kafirun (109), Nasr (110), Lahab (111), Ikhlas (112), Falaq (113), Nas (114)

The Culmination Pyramid

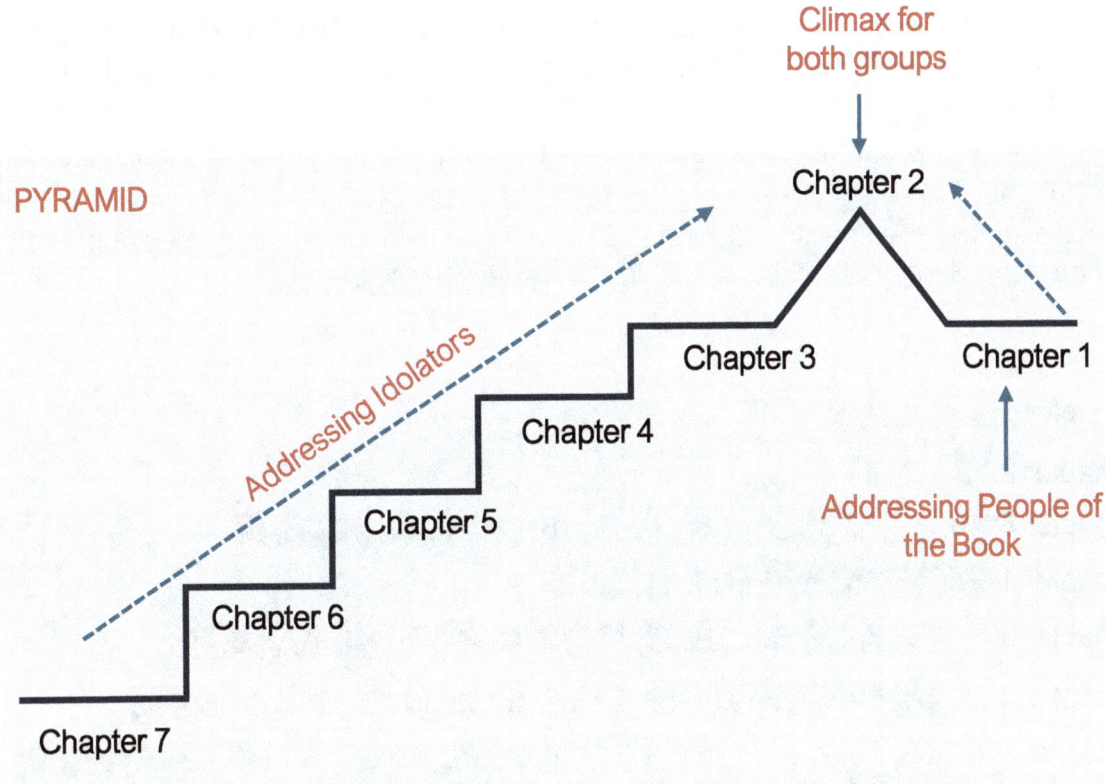

- The culmination of the Prophet's mission is reached in Chapter 2 for the two major groups of the Quran's direct addressees.
- Hypocrites and the People of the Book are the main addressees of Chapter 1, and Idolaters, primarily, are the addressees of Chapters 3-7.
- In this culmination, the verdict against each group, including Muslims, is given.
- The illustration shows the culminating path and the irregular pyramid formed by the chapters.
- In Chapters 3-7, the people of the book are addressed, but in the context of the Idolaters.
- Similarly, in Chapter 1, the idolaters are addressed, but in the context of the people of the book.

Surahs related to the Phases

- The Surahs in each chapter that belong to a specific phase of the mission are marked.
- Compare this with the table that shows the distribution of Makki and Medani Surahs in each chapter. The Medani Surahs are enclosed in a box ⬚ the rest are Makki Surahs.
- This will help you understand that most of the early phases are described in the Makki Surahs.
- For example, the specific warning to Quraysh and their associated tribes appeared in chapter 6 Surahs 50-56 in Makkah (50, 51, 52, 53, 54, 55, 56)

Chapter 1: 1, 2, 3, 4, 5

Chapter 2: 6, 7, 8, 9

Chapter 3: 10, 11, 12, 13, 14, 15, 16, 17, 18, 19, 20, 21, 22, 23, 24

Chapter 4: 25, 26, 27, 28, 29, 30, 31, 32, 33

Chapter 5: 34, 35, 36, 37, 38, 39, 40, 41, 42, 43, 44, 45, 46, 47, 48, 49

Chapter 6: 50, 51, 52, 53, 54, 55, 56, 57, 58, 59, 60, 61, 62, 63, 64, 65, 66

Chapter 7: 67, 68, 69, 70, 71, 72, 73, 74, 75, 76, 77, 78, 79, 80, 81, 82, 83, 84, 85, 86, 87, 88, 89, 90, 91, 92, 93, 94, 95, 96, 97, 98, 99, 100, 101, 102, 103, 104, 105, 106, 107, 108, 109, 110, 111, 112, 113, 114

Commissioning	1
Specific Warning	6
General Warning	37
Completion of Arguments	31
Migration and Cutting Ties	16
Purification and selection	15
Reward and Punishment	2

⬚ Medani Surahs

Assignments

Print a copy of pages 16-19 and keep it with a copy of the Quran. Next time you read the Quran, consider these main themes and phases.

Find one Surah in each group in Juzz number 30, which covers the following phases:

1. Phase of Migration & Acquittal (*Hijrah wa Bara'ah*)
2. Phase of Presenting the Public Warning to Everyone

Confirm that the topic of the Surah aligns with the theme of the phase.

Chapter 8

The Quran and Other Scriptures

In this chapter, we will discuss the relationship between the Quran and the other religious scriptures in the Abrahamic tradition.

The Timeline of Scriptures

- The Quran is not the first book of Islam; it is the last. A brief history is given below.

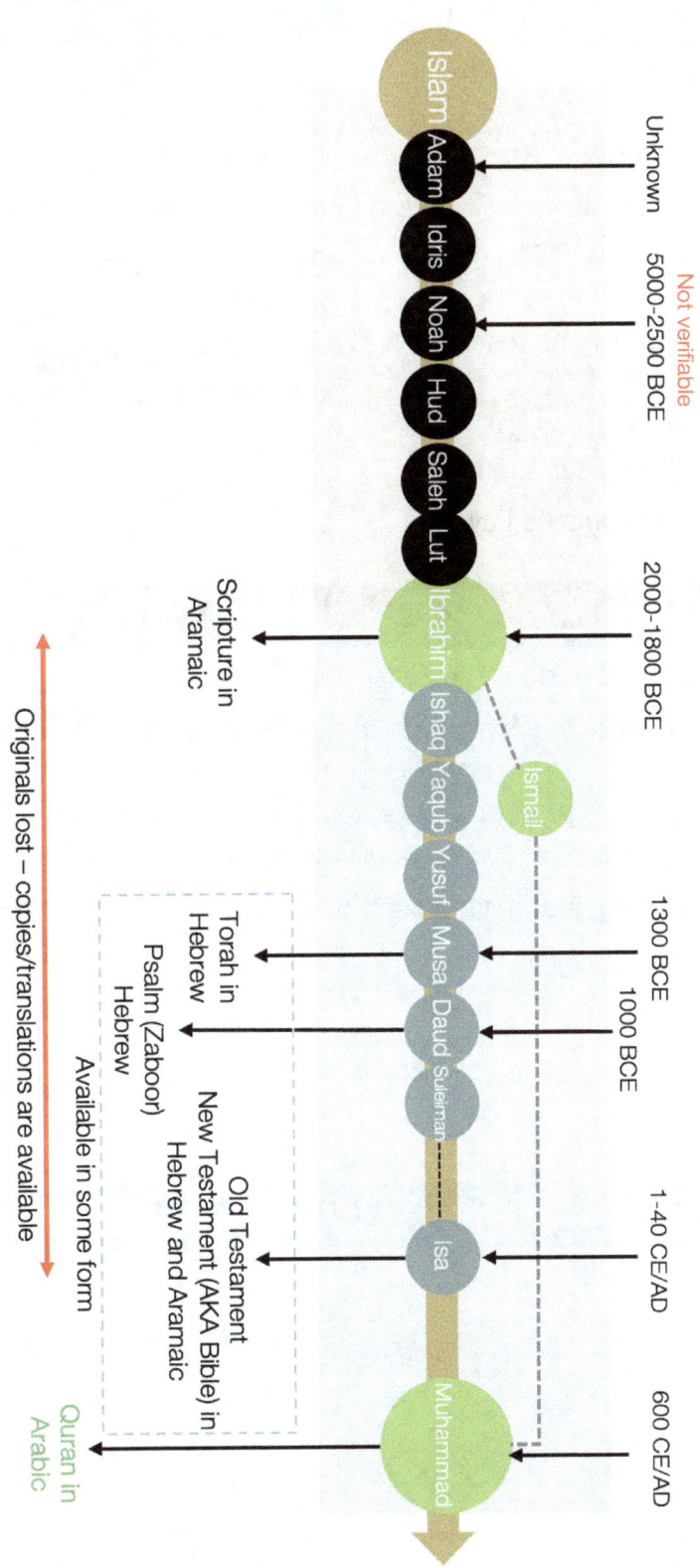

Other Divine Books

Torah

- Revealed to Musa and is also called "The Old Testament."
- Composed of the first 5 books of the Bible, called the Pentateuch.
- The original is lost, then probably again compiled in the 5th century BC
- The Hebrew text is found in manuscripts (Masoretic Text).
- There are other variants, also with important differences between them.
- The majority of the text contains **Law**

Psalms

- Revealed to Dawud and is also called "Psalms of David".
- Collection of Hymns.
- Five books and 150 Psalms.
- Psalms related to other people all made their way into the collection
- It is mostly the **praises of God** and the wisdom behind the religion.

Gospels

- Revealed to Jesus and are part of "The New Testament".
- Gospel means "good news" and was given to the last prophet of the children of Israel.
- The Gospels could not be compiled, so they were narrated by the disciples of Jesus – 4 of them were selected (Matthew, Mark, Luke, and John).
- Originally written in Greek, but the language of Jesus is known to be Aramaic
- It contains the **wisdom of religion.**

Current Bible = Torah + Psalms + Gospels + History

The Quran contains all three subjects in its ultimate form

Scriptures of the Abrahamic Tradition

- Originally, Torah, the Bible, and the Psalms were divine scriptures. However, we must distinguish between the original revelations and the current physical texts of these scriptures, which most Islamic scholars believe have been subject to human modifications and historical changes.
- Despite the additions and modifications, the part of the scripture that is associated with Moses and Jesus, not the historical, still contains traces of the true teachings of Moses and Jesus.
- The Torah is included in the Bible as the "Old Testament."
- The entire Bible is not considered "revealed" – the revealed text is part of the Bible.
- Most of the Bible is history written by the followers of Jesus – the Torah, Psalms, and Gospels (the revealed texts) make up a tiny portion of the Bible.
- The history <u>must not be considered </u>part of the revealed text. However, the People of the Book regard the entire Bible, including its historical accounts, as sacred.
- All interpolations are made in the historical text; the revealed text is somewhat free from these interpolations.
- Most historical and revealed texts underwent revisions.
- When the Quran mentions these Scriptures, it does not refer to the entire Bible, but rather to the revealed text.
- The teachings of the revealed text are closely aligned with those of the Quran.

https://medium.com/@gravitterkaya/the-bible-was-not-always-what-it-is-a-timeline-of-changes-through-history-08f306f7fde7

Quran about other Scriptures

- According to the Quran, three sources precede it as sources of guidance: innate guidance (Fitrah), the Sunnah of Prophet Ibrahim, and the previous Scriptures.
- When it comes to previous Scriptures, there is still a rich treasure of laws and wisdom.
- God used the guidance and the news of the coming of Prophet Muhammad in the Torah and the Gospel as evidence against the People of the Book before punishing them.
- Before the punishment, God at times asked them to follow their own books (they were guilty of not even following their own).

- God praised some of them who used to recite their own books at night during prayers.
- When the Quran challenges their beliefs, it asks them to provide evidence from the Torah and the Gospels to support their claims.
- All of the above remained true until the period of warning and argument was over, and God announced punishment for the People of the Book at the hands of Prophet Muhammad and his companions.

نَزَّلَ عَلَيْكَ الْكِتَابَ بِالْحَقِّ مُصَدِّقاً لِّمَا بَيْنَ يَدَيْهِ وَأَنْزَلَ التَّوْرَاةَ وَالْإِنْجِيلَ مِن قَبْلُ هُدًى لِّلنَّاسِ وَأَنْزَلَ الْفُرْقَانَ إِنَّ الَّذِينَ كَفَرُواْ بِآيَاتِ اللهِ لَهُمْ عَذَابٌ شَدِيدٌ وَاللهُ عَزِيزٌ ذُو انتِقَامٍ

[O Prophet!], He has revealed to you the Book with the truth, in confirmation of the scriptures which preceded it; before this, He has already revealed the Torah and the Gospel <u>for the guidance of mankind</u>, and [after them] revealed this Furqan. Indeed, those who deny God's revelations shall be sternly punished; God is mighty and capable of retribution. (3:3-4)

إِنَّا أَنْزَلْنَا التَّوْرٰىةَ فِيْهَا هُدًى وَّ نُوْرٌ ۚ يَحْكُمُ بِهَا النَّبِيُّوْنَ الَّذِيْنَ أَسْلَمُوْا لِلَّذِيْنَ هَادُوْا وَ الرَّبّٰنِيُّوْنَ وَ الْأَحْبَارُ بِمَا اسْتُحْفِظُوْا مِنْ كِتٰبِ اللهِ وَ كَانُوْا عَلَيْهِ شُهَدَآءَ

We have revealed this Torah, in which **there was both guidance and light**. Through it, the obedient prophets of God, the rabbis, and the jurists would deliver verdicts for these Jews because they had been made custodians of this Book of God and witnesses to it. (5:44)

وَ قَفَّيْنَا عَلٰى اٰثَارِهِمْ بِعِيْسَى ابْنِ مَرْيَمَ مُصَدِّقًا لِّمَا بَيْنَ يَدَيْهِ مِنَ التَّوْرٰىةِ ۚ وَ اٰتَيْنٰهُ الْإِنْجِيْلَ فِيْهِ هُدًى وَّ نُوْرٌ ۙ وَّ مُصَدِّقًا لِّمَا بَيْنَ يَدَيْهِ مِنَ التَّوْرٰىةِ وَ هُدًى وَّ مَوْعِظَةً لِّلْمُتَّقِيْنَ

In the footsteps of these [messengers], We sent forth Jesus, son of Mary, who corroborated the present Torah. And We gave him the Gospel in which **there was guidance and light**. It also corroborated the Torah that was present before it as a guide and an admonition for the God-fearing, with the directive. (5:46)

وَ لَقَدْ كَتَبْنَا فِى الزَّبُوْرِ مِنْ بَعْدِ الذِّكْرِ اَنَّ الْأَرْضَ يَرِثُهَا عِبَادِىَ الصّٰلِحُوْنَ

We had written in the Psalms after the reminder that [on that day] the earth [that will come into existence] shall be inherited by My righteous servants. (21:105)

وَأَنزَلْنَا إِلَيْكَ الْكِتَابَ بِالْحَقِّ مُصَدِّقًا لِّمَا بَيْنَ يَدَيْهِ مِنَ الْكِتَابِ وَمُهَيْمِنًا عَلَيْهِ ۖ فَاحْكُم بَيْنَهُم بِمَا أَنزَلَ اللَّهُ ۖ وَلَا تَتَّبِعْ أَهْوَاءَهُمْ عَمَّا جَاءَكَ مِنَ الْحَقِّ

And [O Prophet!] We have revealed the Book with the truth, confirming it before it and standing as a guardian over it. Therefore, give judgment among them according to the guidance revealed by God and do not yield to their whims by swerving from the truth revealed to you. (5:48)

God called the Quran *Muhaymin* over other divine books, which means the Guardian or Protector

All religious texts of other Divine Books must be understood in the light of the Quran if the Quran covers that topic

Quran and Bible – Relationship

- The Quran omits many historical details in the stories of the prophets, assuming that its addressees are familiar with them from their scriptures.
- The Bible contains numerous detailed stories because it comprises 'revealed texts' with extensive Jewish history.
- Scholars of Islam have been using the Bible as a supplementary source of information or for details of specific incidents that the Quran is not explicit about.
- The Quran avoids purely historical stories; it presents history to support an argument or provide evidence, and it refrains from unnecessary detail (the story of Ashab al Kahf in the Quran is an excellent example of this).
- Muslims should study other scriptures in light of the Quran and under the guidance of a teacher – matters of faith and law should be taken ONLY from the Quran.

Read the story of Joseph (Prophet Yusuf) in the Bible and the Quran and create a comparative table with differences.

Chapter 9

Huroof Al-Muqatta'at (Disjointed Letters)

In this chapter, we will discuss the Disjointed Letters (also known as Huroof Al-Muqatta'at) in the Quran.

Huroof Muqattaat Disjointed Letters

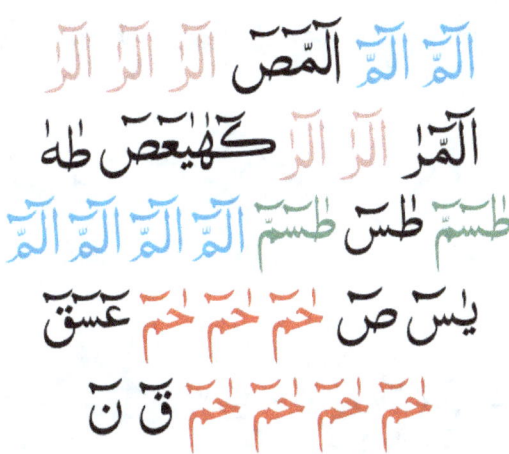

- Many Surahs of the Quran start with certain letters, written alone or together, but they are disjointed and do not form a word.
- A large number of scholarly books have been written over the centuries on the possible meaning and significance of these letters, with no conclusion.
- It is interesting to note that no companion or disbeliever at the time inquired about it with the Prophet Muhammad, suggesting that it was well known in Arabic literature.
- If grouped together, there are around 15 different opinions about these letters.
- Some groups of Muslims have associated "secret" meanings with them, known to a few people, "closer" to Allah.
- Some assurance or emphasis comes from Allah after these letters in most of the Surah (examples in the next slide).

Their usage in the Quran

الٓرٰ تِلْكَ اٰيٰتُ الْكِتٰبِ الْمُبِيْنِ

الٓمٓ ۚ ذٰلِكَ الْكِتٰبُ لَا رَيْبَ ۛ

These are the verses of the Book that state its intent with full clarity.

This is the Book of God. There is no doubt that it is the Book of God.

الٓمٓصٓ ۚ كِتٰبٌ اُنْزِلَ اِلَيْكَ فَلَا يَكُنْ فِيْ صَدْرِكَ حَرَجٌ مِّنْهُ

This Book has been revealed to you, so [O Prophet!] let not there be any anxiety in your heart because of it

الٓمّٓ ۚ اَحَسِبَ النَّاسُ اَنۡ یُّتۡرَكُوۡۤا اَنۡ یَّقُوۡلُوۡۤا اٰمَنَّا وَ هُمۡ لَا یُفۡتَنُوۡنَ

Have people thought that they will be left alone merely because of saying: "We believed," and they will not be put through a test?

كٓهٰیٰعٓصٓ ۚ ذِكۡرُ رَحۡمَتِ رَبِّكَ عَبۡدَهٗ زَكَرِیَّا

This is a mention of the blessings and mercy of your Lord, which He had bestowed on His servant Zacharias.

الٓمّٓ ۚ غُلِبَتِ الرُّوۡمُ ۙ فِیۡۤ اَدۡنَی الۡاَرۡضِ وَ هُمۡ مِّنۡۢ بَعۡدِ غَلَبِهِمۡ سَیَغۡلِبُوۡنَ

The Romans have been defeated in the nearby land, but after this defeat of theirs, they shall soon be victorious.

Some popular opinions

- Somehow, the names of Allah are hidden in these letters when joined in different combinations.
- These are different names of the Quran.
- These are "mysterious" letters, and only God knows their meaning.
- By counting and summing the numerical values of these letters through the science of numerology, the time for doomsday and the age of humanity can be determined.
- These are the first letters of the words of a sentence.
- These letters have healing powers.
- These are the names of the Surahs.
- These are the names of the Surahs and represent objects (living or non-living) that are mentioned in the Surah (Maulana Hamid Uddin Farahi).

At best, these letters are on the topic of *Mutashabihaat* in the Quran. Regarding *Mutashabihaat*, we are asked not to investigate them, as it will be a futile attempt

Most plausible explanation

These are the names of the Surahs, which are categorized based on the topic covered in each Surah. In ancient Arabic and other languages, letters were used to represent things (Research of Hamid Uddin Farahi)

In ancient languages, the symbol for "noon" is a fish. Surah "Noon" talks about Prophet Yunus and the fish

In ancient languages, the symbol of "Taa" represents a snake. Surah "Ta ha" talks about Prophet Musa and the snake

- Amin Ahsan Islahi (1904-1997), a renowned student of Farahi, has mentioned that since Arabs once used such letters in their poetry, it was only fitting for the Quran to adopt the same style. That's why they did not raise any objection to these letters.
- This area remains a subject of ongoing research, and scholars consistently encourage new studies on this topic.

The misconceptions
(deviations)

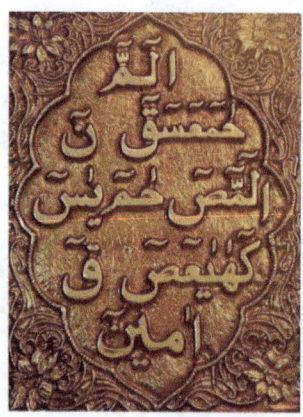

- In 1974, an Egyptian biochemist named Rashad Khalifa claimed to have discovered a mathematical code in the Quran based on these initials and the number 19, which is mentioned in Sura 74:30 ("19 angles guard the hell fire"). According to his claims, these initials occur throughout their respective chapters in multiples of nineteen. He has noted other mathematical phenomena throughout the Quran, all related to what he describes as the "mathematical miracle of the Quran."

- The *Loh-e-Qurani* (inscribed on a metallic tablet) is considered a sacred object in Islamic tradition, and some believe it possesses mystical powers. It is often used in religious ceremonies, such as reciting Quranic verses or performing prayers, for meditation and spiritual healing. People hang them on walls in their homes for protection and as a symbol of blessings.

Read as many Surahs of the Quran that start with Huroof Al Muqatta'at and find a pattern from the verses right after them or the topic covered in that Surah. Present your research.

Chapter 10

Oaths in the Quran

In this chapter, we will discuss the use of Oaths in the Quran and why its style is unique in this regard.

The Purpose of the Oaths

- In the Quran, God Almighty has sworn by Himself and by many of His creations to affirm a claim-statement.

- Scholars of the Quran have debated the nature, significance, and wisdom behind these oaths – some have referred to them as Mutashabihaat, whose meaning is known only to God.

- Three main questions have been raised (some critics of the Quran have raised them as objections) by almost every careful reader of the Quranic text, as the human reason inspires them.

  - Oaths are taken to emphasize and register the truth of one's statement by invoking someone who is a higher being, nobler and more respected than the oath-taker. Oaths are conventionally sworn by taking the name of sacred objects. However, in the Quran, God swears by ordinary and insignificant things on many occasions. It does not match God's exalted position.

  - God has taken oaths to affirm fundamental Islamic beliefs, such as monotheism, the Day of Judgment, and prophethood. To non-believers, these beliefs cannot be imposed by the mere sanctity of an oath unless they are established independently for them first. In other words, the oaths appear to be a fruitless insistence only.

  - Islam has taught believers not to swear by anything other than the Glorious God, but God has taken oaths of cities, fruits, the sun, and the moon.

- **Components:** The verse or verses that contain the oath have two components right after the letter of the oath. These two components are **swear-by and swear-for.** The object sworn by is called the _Muqsam Bihi_, and the statement or truth for which the oath is taken is known as the _Muqsam Alayh_.

- In the example below, the letter of oath is "wow" وَ

Muqsam Bihi	This is the entity or thing by which the oath is sworn.
Muqsam Alayh	This is the statement or the truth that is being emphasized by the oath.

وَ التِّيْنِ وَ الزَّيْتُوْنِ وَ طُوْرِ سِيْنِيْنَ وَ هٰذَا الْبَلَدِ الْأَمِيْنِ   _Muqsam Bihi (Swear by)_

لَقَدْ خَلَقْنَا الْإِنْسَانَ فِيْ اَحْسَنِ تَقْوِيْمٍ ثُمَّ رَدَدْنٰهُ اَسْفَلَ سٰفِلِيْنَ   _Muqsam Alayh (Swear for)_

Relationship between Swear-by and Swear-for

- If oaths are taken merely for emphasis, then they fail to address the question of the relationship between the Swear by and Swear for – for example, Quran 68:1-2, 100:1-6, 103:1-2.
- One of the greatest Islamic scholars of the 20th century, Imam Hamid Uddin Farahi, considers these oaths as evidence (something bearing witness) presented by God to establish a fact, not just an emphasis.
- Swear-by furnishes evidence or becomes a witness for Swear for.
- Linguistically, the particles of the oath are ba', waw, and ta'. ب و ن
- Oaths are an instrument of Quranic logic and reasoning, and there is no reason to emphasize the greatness of the Swear by (it can be the sun or the moon or fighting horses, etc).
- There are multiple types of oaths (or Swear by) in the Quran:

Phenomenal Oath	Historical Oath
Multiple phenomena of nature are sworn by	Cites one or more events from the past

Experiential Oath	Conjugate Oath
Certain aspect of human experience is presented as evidence	One member of a pair is discussed, and the other member is cited as evidence

Examples from the Quran
Phenomenal Oath

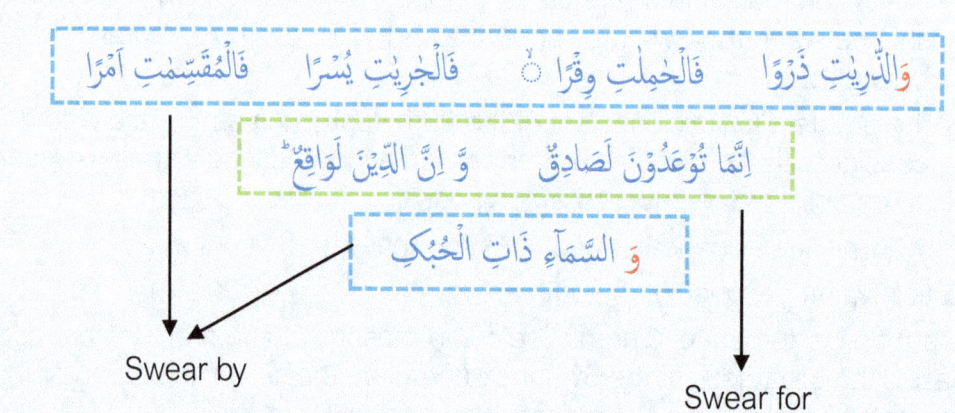

Swear by

Swear for

Fierce winds that scatter dust lift clouds filled with rain, then glide slowly, then distribute matters differently [bear witness] together with the striped sky that the punishment you are being threatened with is true, and indeed reward and punishment shall certainly take place.
(Surah Dhariat:1-7)

- This premise is substantiated by the multifarious effects of winds. The implication is that, many times in history, people have witnessed winds bring forth clouds and rain down on rebellious nations, destroying them in an instant. In the past, such winds became a source of mercy, blessing, and a means of salvation from enemies. Thus, if the people of the Quraysh have a vision, they can see that even now, these incidents of reward and punishment, which were caused by the winds and clouds, bear evidence that both the punishment, as well as the day of judgment, whose warnings are being sounded to them, are bound to come.

Examples from the Quran Historical Oath

| وَ التِّيْنِ وَ الزَّيْتُوْنِ   وَ طُوْرِ سِيْنِيْنَ   وَ هٰذَا الْبَلَدِ الْأَمِيْنِ | Swear by |

| لَقَدْ خَلَقْنَا الْإِنْسَانَ فِيْ اَحْسَنِ تَقْوِيْمٍ ثُمَّ رَدَدْنٰهُ اَسْفَلَ سٰفِلِيْنَ | Swear for |

The (mount of) figs and olives and the mount of Sinai and this peaceful city bear witness that We have created man in the finest of molds (best nation), and then We reverted him to the lowest position (disgraced the nation because of their actions) (Surah Teen: 1-5)

Historical Reference

(mount of) figs and olives	⟶	Place refers to Jesus
Mount of Sinai	⟶	Place refers to Moses
This peaceful city	⟶	Place refers to Ibrahim

- These three places (mount of Olive, mount of Sinai, and City of Makkah) are evidence that human beings were created on the straight path, were monotheists, had a strong belief in the Hereafter, and were morally upright, but when they deviated from the straight path and did not follow their good instinct given to them by God then they fell into the pit of disgrace.

Examples from the Quran
Experiential Oath

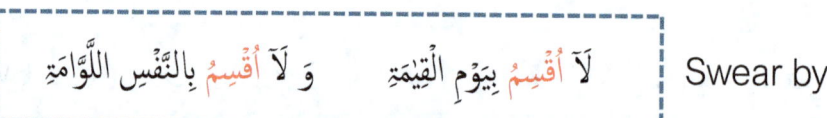 Swear by

(They reject the Day of Judgment), by no means, I swear by the Day of Judgment, and I swear by the rebuking soul … (Surah Qiyamah: 1-2)

- Swear-for is hidden, but the next verse provides the hint, as shown below.

اَيَحۡسَبُ الۡاِنۡسَانُ اَلَّنۡ نَّجۡمَعَ عِظَامَهٗ   بَلٰى قٰدِرِيۡنَ عَلٰٓى اَنۡ نُّسَوِّىَ بَنَانَهٗ

Does man think that We will not be able to bring together his bones? Why not! We can even put the sections of his fingers together. (Surah Qiyamah: 3)

- When a particle of negation occurs before an oath, it is meant to refute a notion of the addressee for whose refutation the oath had been sworn in or evidence had been presented. In our language, we say the same thing: "No, by God, that is not true." In these verses, the swear-for is hidden because the swear-by is so powerful and evident towards the swear-for that there is no need to mention it. Secondly, the evidence of a rebuking soul inside every human being points to the Day of Judgment and makes the swear-for very obvious.

Examples from the Quran
Conjugate Oath

وَ الشَّمْسِ وَ ضُحٰىهَا ۞ وَ الْقَمَرِ اِذَا تَلٰىهَا ۞ وَ النَّهَارِ اِذَا جَلّٰىهَا ۞ وَ الَّيْلِ اِذَا يَغْشٰىهَا

وَ السَّمَآءِ وَ مَا بَنٰىهَا ۞ وَ الْاَرْضِ وَ مَا طَحٰىهَا ۞ وَ نَفْسٍ وَّ مَا سَوّٰىهَا

فَاَلْهَمَهَا فُجُوْرَهَا وَ تَقْوٰىهَا ۞ قَدْ اَفْلَحَ مَنْ زَكّٰىهَا ۞ وَ قَدْ خَابَ مَنْ دَسّٰىهَا

And by the sun and its brightness (in the day), and by the moon as it follows it (the sun), And by the day as it shows up (the sun's) brightness, and by the night as it conceals it (the sun), and by the heaven as it was built, and by the earth as it was spread, and by the human soul as it was perfected, then revealed to him the goodness and evil. (that the Day of Judgment or Hereafter is going to happen) Then indeed he succeeds who purifies his soul, and indeed he fails who corrupts his soul (Surah Shams:1-10)

Many things to Swear by, but Swear for is hidden

- Seemingly opposite but complementary phenomena are presented as evidence for God to bring a Day or a Universe that should be complementary to this world.
- This is a very common style in the Quran, in which it presents an argument in favor of the Day of Judgment.
- The Hereafter is the missing pair of this Life.

Identify the Swear for in the following Surahs:
- Surah An-Najm
- Surah At-Tariq
- Surah Al-Burooj

Resources

https://www.javedahmadghamidi.com/quran-home
https://www.tafheem.net/

Chapter 11

The Quran and Science

In this chapter, we will discuss the relationship between the Quran and Science (if any) and the best approach to look at this matter.

The purpose of the Quran

- The Quran is the book of God, and He reveals its purpose to us.
- The purpose of the Quran is already mentioned multiple times by God in the Quran.

صٓ وَ الْقُرْاٰنِ ذِى الذِّكْرِ

This is Surah Suad. By the Quran, replete with **reminders** (full of reminders) (38:1)

ذٰلِكَ الْكِتٰبُ لَا رَيْبَ فِيْهِ هُدًى لِّلْمُتَّقِيْنَ

This is the Book of God. There is no doubt in it being the Book of God. It is **guidance** for the God-fearing. (2:2)

فَذَكِّرْ بِالْقُرْاٰنِ مَنْ يَّخَافُ وَعِيْدِ

So, **remind** through this Quran those who fear My warning. (50:45)

كِتٰبٌ اَنْزَلْنٰهُ اِلَيْكَ مُبٰرَكٌ لِّيَدَّبَّرُوْٓا اٰيٰتِهٖ وَ لِيَتَذَكَّرَ اُولُوا الْاَلْبَابِ

It is a blessed book which We have revealed to you [O Prophet] so that people **ponder** on its verses and those endowed with intellect are reminded by it. (38:29)

اَفَمَنْ يَّعْلَمُ اَنَّمَآ اُنْزِلَ اِلَيْكَ مِنْ رَّبِّكَ الْحَقُّ كَمَنْ هُوَ اَعْمٰى ۚ اِنَّمَا يَتَذَكَّرُ اُولُوا الْاَلْبَابِ

So, will the person who knows that whatever has been revealed to you from your Lord is the truth become like the one who is blind? [This is a reminder, and] only they receive a **reminder** who use their intellect (13:19)

سُوْرَةٌ اَنْزَلْنٰهَا وَ فَرَضْنٰهَا وَ اَنْزَلْنَا فِيْهَآ اٰيٰتٍ بَيِّنٰتٍ لَّعَلَّكُمْ تَذَكَّرُوْنَ

This is a grand surah that We have revealed and have made its directives mandatory [upon you] and have also revealed very clear **admonitions** in it so that you take heed. (24:1)

What is the Quran?

In summary, the Quran is a literary masterpiece, and the verses of the Quran are for people to ponder over and act as a reminder for them (for their faith, moral guidance, and accountability on the day of judgment).

Verses of the Quran state physical science

- There are many verses in the Quran in which topics related to the natural sciences are discussed.

ثُمَّ جَعَلْنٰهُ نُطْفَةً فِى قَرَارٍ مَّكِينٍ

ثُمَّ خَلَقْنَا النُّطْفَةَ عَلَقَةً فَخَلَقْنَا الْعَلَقَةَ مُضْغَةً فَخَلَقْنَا الْمُضْغَةَ عِظٰمًا فَكَسَوْنَا الْعِظٰمَ لَحْمًا ثُمَّ اَنْشَاْنٰهُ خَلْقًا اٰخَرَ ۚ

Then, making it into [a dripping] drop of fluid, We placed it in a secure spot. Then We gave this drop of fluid the form of a blood clot, and made the blood clot into a lump of flesh, and created bones in the lump, and covered the bones with flesh. Then, We made it into a new creation altogether. (23:13-14)

وَ الشَّمْسُ تَجْرِىْ لِمُسْتَقَرٍّ لَّهَا ۚ ذٰلِكَ تَقْدِيْرُ الْعَزِيْزِ الْعَلِيْمِ

وَ الْقَمَرَ قَدَّرْنٰهُ مَنَازِلَ حَتّٰى عَادَ كَالْعُرْجُوْنِ الْقَدِيْمِ

لَا الشَّمْسُ يَنْۢبَغِىْ لَهَآ اَنْ تُدْرِكَ الْقَمَرَ وَ لَا الَّيْلُ سَابِقُ النَّهَارِ ۚ وَ كُلٌّ فِىْ فَلَكٍ يَّسْبَحُوْنَ

The sun moves on a prescribed path. This is a measure set by the Powerful and All-Knowing God. And We have appointed phases for the moon until it once again becomes a withered date-twig. Neither can the sun dare catch up with the moon, nor can the night overtake the day. All of them are moving (swimming) along their paths or orbits. (36:38-40)

وَ جَعَلْنَا السَّمَآءَ سَقْفًا مَّحْفُوْظًا	وَ جَعَلْنَا مِنَ الْمَآءِ كُلَّ شَىْءٍ حَىٍّ
And We have made the heavens (sky) a secure roof (21:32)	And We have created every living being with water of the heavens only (21:30)

مَرَجَ الْبَحْرَيْنِ يَلْتَقِيٰنِ ۙ بَيْنَهُمَا بَرْزَخٌ لَّا يَبْغِيٰنِ

He let loose two oceans: both strike one another, yet between them is a barrier that they cannot cross. (55:19-20)

The approaches in interpretation

Approach #1 — Modern scientific discoveries are somehow referenced in the Quran to prove that the Quran is the Word of God.

Approach #2 — When interpreting such verses of the Quran, corroborate them with recent scientific discoveries to the extent possible.

Approach #3 — When interpreting such verses of the Quran, attention must be paid to the words, their usage, and the context in which they are found, regardless of any scientific discoveries associated with them. ✓

Who takes Approach #1 and #2

1. Muslims who are not convinced about Islam need some scientific evidence or proof to be convinced.
2. Muslims who keep looking for more proof to increase their faith in Allah and Islam.
3. A Muslim who thinks that science is the only way to prove in the 21st century that the Quran is the Book of God.
4. Muslims who are the callers to Islam. They use it as an argument to convince their non-Muslim addressees that Islam is a true religion and the Quran is the Book of God.
5. Muslims who have made it a goal of their life to prove that the Quran is a miraculous Book of God.

In a materialistic age, science is highly regarded among the young generation. Muslims who try to prove the Quran through science do so primarily to confirm its divine origin for a modern, scientifically-minded audience.

The dangers of Approaches 1 and 2

- The trend of scientific *tafsir* gained significant momentum in the 14th century AH (20th century CE) as Muslim scholars sought to show that Islam is compatible with modern science.

- It is based on the belief that all branches of human knowledge are found in the Quran, which is not true.

- Science is a body of knowledge that involves dynamic processes where models and theories are developed based on the best available data. These models help us understand the world, but they are always open to revision as new evidence emerges.

- This iterative nature of science is evident from historical shifts:
    - The transition from the geocentric model of the universe to the heliocentric model.
    - From Newtonian physics to Einstein's theory of relativity.

- Each discovery refines our understanding and may replace or modify existing theories, reflecting the evolving nature of scientific knowledge.

- When the scientific knowledge evolves, one of two things must happen:
    - The interpretation of the Quran must change – the critics of the Quran claim that it cannot be a word of God because God is changing His mind, or Muslims don't know what God wants to say.
    - The interpretation of the Quran remains the same – the critics of the Quran claim that it cannot be a word of God because the Quran is entirely against the observable scientific facts.

- This attitude does not help either way.

- The interpretation of the Quranic verses CANNOT evolve with science, as it removes the confidence that a believer has in the Quran, because the word of God cannot change.

- Some of the most famous "Scientific Tafsir" of the Quran are:
    - Tantawi Jawhari (1940)
    - Sayyid Ahmad Khan (19th century)
    - Sayyid Hibatuddin Shahrestani (1967)
    - Allama Muhammad Husayn Tabataba'i (1981)

Claim of Big Bang in the Quran

اَوَ لَمْ يَرَ الَّذِيْنَ كَفَرُوْٓا اَنَّ السَّمٰوٰتِ وَ الْاَرْضَ كَانَتَا رَتْقًا فَفَتَقْنٰهُمَا

Do those who have disbelieved see/realize that the Heavens and the Earth were joined together and We clove them asunder (separated them)? (21:30)

- The above verses are frequently cited in discussions about the universe's origin and expansion, particularly in relation to modern scientific theories, such as the Big Bang and the expanding universe.
- This verse is often interpreted as alluding to the initial singularity and subsequent separation of matter in the Big Bang theory.

Many interpreters and callers to Islam are talking about it

https://www.thelastdialogue.org/article/big-bang-mentioned-in-quran/
https://en.islamonweb.net/big-bang-a-quranic-perspective
https://www.islamreligion.com/articles/1560/quran-on-expanding-universe-and-big-bang-theory

The debate in the scientific community

- Some physicists question what existed before the Big Bang and whether the concept of a singularity (a point of infinite density and temperature) accurately describes the universe's origin (as interpreted from the verse).
- "Despite the continuing popularity of the theory, essentially every prediction of the Big Bang theory has been increasingly contradicted by better and better data, as shown by many teams of researchers." (LPPFusion.com)
- Some critics of the Big Bang theory say it violates the first law of thermodynamics, which states that matter and energy cannot be created or destroyed. Critics claim that the Big Bang theory suggests the universe began out of nothing, which is an unscientific claim

Big Question: How would we interpret this verse if, after 100 years, the scientific community changed its position on the Big Bang due to newer discoveries?

Example 1 – Correct Interpretation

اَوَ لَمْ يَرَ الَّذِيْنَ كَفَرُوْٓا اَنَّ السَّمٰوٰتِ وَ الْاَرْضَ كَانَتَا رَتْقًا فَفَتَقْنٰهُمَا

وَ جَعَلْنَا مِنَ الْمَآءِ كُلَّ شَيْءٍ حَيٍّ ۗ اَفَلَا يُؤْمِنُوْنَ

[They ask for signs.] Have these disbelievers ever seen that the skies and the earth are both closed (sky not raining and earth not producing)? Then We opened them, and We created every living being with water coming only from the sky. Will they even then accept faith? (21:30)

- Before these verses, God scolds the disbelievers for their polytheistic beliefs and asks them for proof.
- He argued that if there are multiple Gods in this universe, they will see chaos in the Skies and on the earth.
- When they asked for proof, God explained that since there is only one God, they could observe that when the Skies are closed, the Earth is also closed, and then He opens them simultaneously. Skies rain, and the earth produces its produce.
- Then He told them how important the water He rains down on earth is for life and sustenance.
- This phenomenon is observable by the disbelievers every day. God is asking them to ponder over it.
- If it were related to the Big Bang, then there was no justification for God asking them to ponder over it because the Bedouins of Arabia had no way of knowing the Big Bang.

Example 2 – Human Embryology

ثُمَّ خَلَقْنَا النُّطْفَةَ عَلَقَةً فَخَلَقْنَا الْعَلَقَةَ مُضْغَةً فَخَلَقْنَا الْمُضْغَةَ عِظَامًا فَكَسَوْنَا الْعِظَامَ لَحْمًا ثُمَّ اَنْشَأْنٰهُ

خَلْقًا اٰخَرَ ۗ فَتَبٰرَكَ اللّٰهُ اَحْسَنُ الْخٰلِقِيْنَ

Then We gave this drop of fluid the form of a blood clot, made the blood clot into a lump of flesh, created bones in the lump, and covered the bones with flesh. Then, We made it into a new creation altogether. So, blessed is God, the best of creators. (23:14)

- Interpreters of the Quran and the callers to Islam claim that the Quran described stages of human development in mothers' wombs, discovered centuries later.
- They claim that modern embryology, through advancements in medical imaging and scientific research, confirms the accuracy of the Quranic descriptions regarding human development. The sequential development of the embryo, as mentioned in the Quran, corresponds remarkably well with contemporary understanding.

https://alhidaayah.com/lessons/lesson-7-embryology/?v=79cba1185463
https://wikiislam.net/wiki/Embryology_in_the_Quran

Critics of the Quran

- Prophet Muhammad plagiarized the work of Hippocrates, Aristotle, and Galen on this, and they were all wrong about human development.
- The meaning of the words '*Alaqah*' and '*Mudgah*' has changed over time. Different interpreters of the Quran assigned different meanings as science progressed, to make it compatible with scientific findings.
- The idea that bones are clothed with flesh is not only scientifically incorrect but also reminiscent of the ancient Greek physician Galen's hypothesis.
- Bone and muscles begin to develop simultaneously rather than sequentially (as the Quran tells us)
- With more scientific research and details emerging, it appears that the sequence of stages mentioned in the Quran is not entirely accurate.

Example 2 – The intent of the verses

- These verses came in the context of disbelievers rejecting the resurrection and the Day of Judgment.
- Combining these specific verses with the verses before and after suggests that God wanted to make a point: if He could create you from nothing (which is more difficult), why can't He create you the second time?
- The stages mentioned in the verses primarily illustrate the grand power of God, who begins with something so insignificant as to form a human being, and later creates giants like Aristotle and Einstein.
- Whether some of the stages occur sequentially or simultaneously is not important here.
- Remember, God is not authoring a book of Anatomy but a book of guidance, in which He uses every conceivable argument to deliver the truth about human resurrection and accountability.
- When interpreting such verses, attention must be paid to the main idea and theme in which these verses are revealed.
- If the verses of the Quran corroborate with the scientific discoveries, then it's a bonus, not the target.

Why does the Quran state scientific phenomena?

Quran's central message
1. There is only one God, and He is the Creator of everything. We and everything in this world are His creations, and He runs all the affairs of this world alone
2. This life is a test that will end one day, called the Day of Judgment. The Day of Judgment is as real and certain as our life
3. On that day, people will be held accountable for their knowledge and deeds in this life, and they will be rewarded with a second life based on the results of their actions

- God presents various pieces of evidence to support His case, including evidence within ourselves, evidence from the outside world, and historical evidence.
- God mentions scientific phenomena when presenting evidence from within and outside of ourselves for any of the above.
- God also mentions scientific phenomena when He wants to demonstrate His power and grandeur in this universe, because for a 7th-century person, these phenomena are observable yet still wonderful (even for us today).

Book of science or a literary masterpiece

- Look at these statements that appear in the Quran and see if they are written from a scientific perspective.

1. Dhul-Qarnayn reached a place where the sun sets; he saw that it was setting into a pond of black mud (18:86).
2. Heavens and earth are created in six 'days', and it did not cause any sense of weariness for God (50:38).
3. He has made the moon a light and the sun a lamp (71:16).
4. God has created night and day, the sun and the moon, each traveling in an orbit (21:33).
5. God raised the skies without pillars (or pillars that you cannot see) (13:2).
6. God could cause a piece of sky to fall upon disbelievers (34:9).
7. On the Day of Judgment, God would roll up the skies and the earth like a written scroll (21:104).
8. Every animate or inanimate object, even the shadows, prostrates to God (16:48).
9. God is the Lord of two Easts and two Wests (55:17).
10. God created everything in pairs as a reminder for the Day of Judgment (51:49).
11. God made the earth flat like a carpet or bed, and the sky a ceiling (2:22).

None of the above statements is scientifically correct

Identify three additional verses of the Quran that mention science. Compare the translations of the Quran done by various interpreters. Give references.

Chapter 12

Understanding the Quran

In this chapter, we will discuss the approach that one should take to understand the Quran.

1. Quran's main message is very simple

- In this chapter, we will discuss some considerations for understanding the Quran.
- Scholars of the Quran agree that there are two levels of understanding.
  - The Quran is the easiest book for a common reader to grasp the main message of Islam, thanks to its simplicity and frequent reminders.
  - On the other hand, it is the most challenging book for scholars who want to delve deeper into understanding the wisdom behind its choice of words, brevity, and relevance until the Day of Judgment.
- The Quran's central message is very simple and can be summarized in three bullet points:

1 There is one true God, and He has no partners. He is the Creator, and we are His creations. He controls everything.

2 This is a temporary life, and a new life will begin after this world is ended, and a new world will be created

3 We will be held accountable for our beliefs and actions, one day, based on the universal innate concepts of good and evil

- Every human being can get this message from the Quran without any effort.
- A simple translation from any mainstream interpreter of the Quran can convey this message repeatedly.
- No scholarly discussions are required to get this message.
- No one could present an excuse on the Day of Judgment that the Quran was difficult, and he/she could not understand its message or what God wants from them.

2. Quran is revealed in Classical Arabic Language

- The Quran was revealed in classical Arabic, the language spoken in Makkah, during the age of Jahiliyyah (the age of ignorance, characterized by tribal mentality before the Prophet), to the tribe of Quraysh.

- A deeper and more accurate understanding of this book depends on a sound knowledge and true appreciation of this language.

- It is quite logical that the book sent to people must be in the language that they are comfortable with, so they can fully benefit from it.

- The words, sentences, idioms, style, and construction cannot be compared with those of today's Arabic language, which Arabs speak today.

فَإِنَّمَا يَسَّرْنَاهُ بِلِسَانِكَ لِتُبَشِّرَ بِهِ الْمُتَّقِينَ وَتُنذِرَ بِهِ قَوْمًا لُّدًّا

Thus, We have made this [Quran] **very easy** and apt in your own tongue that through it you may proclaim glad tidings to the upright and fully warn the stubborn. (19:97)

Walid ibn al-Mughirah, one of the finest critics of the language in Makkah at that time, heard the Quran for the very first time, and his response was:

By God! No one among you is more aware than I of poetry, neither warlike songs nor eulogies nor the incantation of the jinn. By God! The words spoken by this person (Muhammad) resemble none of these. By God! It is very pleasant and lively. Its branches are laden with fruit. Its roots are well-watered. It will definitely dominate [every other thing], and nothing will be able to dominate it, and it will crush everything below it.

3. Quran explains itself

- The Quran presents its message in various ways and styles. As a result, it has become unparalleled among other works in its ability to explain its own verses.
- The same topic appears in various surahs with different details – this is not mere repetition.
- The background, context, and details vary across different places for the same incident.
- In some places, the description is concise, and the matter is only alluded to, and in other places, the details of that matter are revealed.
- At one point, a word is unclear, but at another, its usage hints at how it was used originally.
- The emphasis and perspective on the same event differ from place to place.

وَلَقَدْ صَرَّفْنَا فِي هَذَا الْقُرْآنِ لِيَذَّكَّرُواْ

We have explained this in the Quran in multiple ways, so that they take heed (17:41)

اللَّهُ نَزَّلَ أَحْسَنَ الْحَدِيثِ كِتَابًا مُّتَشَابِهًا مَّثَانِيَ

God has revealed the best discourse whose verses resemble one another and whose surahs occur in pairs. (39:23)

كِتَابٌ أُحْكِمَتْ آيَاتُهُ ثُمَّ فُصِّلَتْ مِن لَّدُنْ حَكِيمٍ خَبِيرٍ

This is a Book whose verses were first concise, then explained by Him, who is wise and all-knowing. (11:1)

A principle agreed upon by the scholars of the Quran

الْقُرْآنُ يُفَسِّرُ بَعْضُهُ بَعْضاً

The Quran explains itself

The best way to understand the Quran is to look at all the verses in the Quran related to that topic

4. Generic and Specific

- General and specific verses should be differentiated
- There are many places in the Quran where the words are general; however, the context testifies with complete certainty that something specific is meant
- For example, the Quran uses the word An'naas (people), but it ← النَّاس
  does not refer to all the people of the world; often, they do not
  even refer to all the people of Arabia: the word refers to a
  group among them.
- It uses the expression Alad Deeni Kullihi (over all the religions), ← عَلَى الدِّيْنِ كُلِّهِ
  and it does not refer to all religions of the world
- It refers to Al-Mushrikun (the polytheists), but they do not refer ← المُشْرِكُوْن
  to all those who are guilty of polytheism
- Similarly, the words Min Ahl al Kitaab (And from these People of ← مِنْ أَهْلِ الْكِتَابِ
  the Book) do not refer to all the People of the Book of the world
- It mentions the word Insaan (the man), but it does not refer to
  mankind, but a group of people ← الإِنْسَان

Reasoning of Revelation (Asbaab un Nuzool)

- There is a general understanding among Muslims that the "reasoning, occasion, and circumstances" of many Quranic verses (called Asbaab un Nuzool or Shaan e Nuzool) are known through Ahadith, and that it is important to take them into account when understanding the Quran.
- Since the Quran explains itself and the background, context, and stage of the Prophet's mission can be determined within it, there is no reason to rely solely on an external source to explain why the verses were revealed.
- It is generally misunderstood that these narrations indicate the reason for revelation; at most, they describe the occasion and circumstances under which a particular group of verses was revealed, or a particular directive was given, as should be understood from the Quran.
- The occasion and circumstances in which a verse or a group of verses was revealed are usually determined by the stage of Prophet Muhammad's mission, which is quite evident within a Surah.

5. The meaning of a word

The meaning of a word is determined:

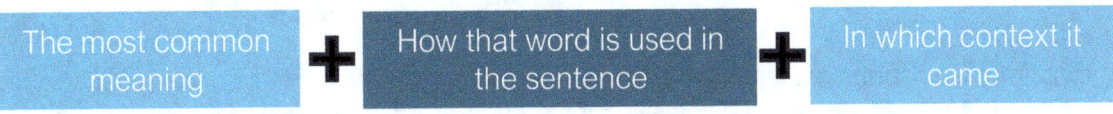

| The most common meaning | **+** | How that word is used in the sentence | **+** | In which context it came |

What does Tiger imply here?

Tipu Sultan, the **Tiger** of Mysore, was the Indian Muslim ruler of the Kingdom of Mysore and was considered a brave leader.

- In this example, the writer has written this sentence to convey a specific message or meaning.
- To convey a message with specific meaning, a three-step process is required:
    - **Analyze Common Usages:** Investigate both the literal and figurative applications of a key word (e.g., "Tiger"). The determination of its intended nature will be informed by the subsequent two steps.
    - **Contextualize Usage:** Ascertain how the word is employed within the specific sentence or phrase, and identify the message it aims to communicate in that context.
    - **Understand Broader Context:** Analyze the surrounding text or statement to fully comprehend the environment in which the sentence or phrase appears.
- Following this comprehensive analysis, it becomes evident that the term "Tiger" is utilized figuratively to commend the renowned bravery of a prominent figure, such as Tipu Sultan.

Example from the Quran

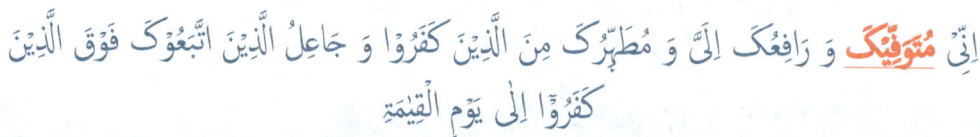

اِنِّى مُتَوَفِّيْكَ وَ رَافِعُكَ اِلَىَّ وَ مُطَهِّرُكَ مِنَ الَّذِيْنَ كَفَرُوْا وَ جَاعِلُ الَّذِيْنَ اتَّبَعُوْكَ فَوْقَ الَّذِيْنَ كَفَرُوْا اِلَى يَوْمِ الْقِيٰمَةِ

At that time, God said: "Jesus, I have <u>decided to give you death</u> and lift you to Myself. I shall purify you from those who have disbelieved in you and grant your followers supremacy over these disbelievers until the Day of Judgement.

Step #1: | The most common meaning |

The word "*Mutawaffa*" is used in the Quran multiple times to mean death. This is the most popular meaning of this word.

Step #2: | How that word is used in the sentence |

Allah is telling Jesus, step by step, what his plan is for him. Raising will occur after he dies

Step #3: | In which context it came

Allah has made such a decision because the Jews have decided to kill him, and Allah's practice is that He does not allow anyone to overpower Messengers

---

Some scholars of the Quran have taken the meaning of *Mutawaffa* as "take someone to yourself," which does not fit well in the sentence

6. Importance of the Context

وَ اعْتَصِمُوا بِحَبْلِ اللهِ جَمِيعًا وَّ لَا تَفَرَّقُوا

And hold firmly to the rope of Allah (the Quran) all together and do not become divided (3:103)

- Turning to the Quran to resolve all disagreements is possible only when its verdict is clear and unambiguous.
- There is a general misunderstanding that the verses of the Quran have multiple meanings, and it is evident that many interpretations of each verse exist (some even contradictory to one another).
- If a difference of opinion arises in the interpretation of a discourse, the most satisfactory way to resolve this is through the context and coherence of the discourse.
- Many differences of opinion have arisen in understanding Islam because of disregard for the context of a verse. If this context is taken into consideration, one will find that, in most cases, only one interpretation is possible (in that context).
- What makes the Quran a document having one definite meaning and which resolves all differences of interpretation is the CONTEXT of the verse.

الْقُرْآنُ لَا يَحْتَمِلُ إِلاَّ تَأْوِيْلاً وَاحِداً

"There is no possibility of more than one interpretation in the Quran." (a famous quote of Iman Hamid Uddin Farahi, a Quran Scholar)

7. Relationship between Quran and Hadith

God has revealed with truth the Book, **which is this scale** [of criterion]. (42:17)

Blessed be He who has revealed **Al Furqan (the criterion)** to His servant that it may warn the whole world. (25:1)

- There is a common misconception that certain Ahadith cancel or supersede specific Quranic instructions.
- If this is considered accurate, then there is no reason to believe that the Quran is the final authority, the scale, and the criterion of religion.
- The Quran is the standard by which everything else is judged as right or wrong.
- The Quran is a **<u>Furqan</u>** in the same sense, i.e., a book with the final and absolute verdict to distinguish between truth and falsehood.
- It is the Quran, its words, sentence structure, and the context that will decide what God wants to say.
- The Prophet did three things in his lifetime:
    - Delivered the Quran
    - Established the Sunnah
    - Explained the implied meanings in the verses of the Quran, which were not stated in words and required some deliberation
- Examining those Ahadith, it is clear that when people were unable to comprehend certain stylistic features of the Quran, including its background and perspective, they also struggled to understand the Prophet's words on these topics.

Example of Implied Meaning

يَا أَيُّهَا الَّذِينَ آمَنُوا كُلُوا مِنْ طَيِّبَاتِ مَا رَزَقْنَاكُمْ وَ اشْكُرُوا لِلَّهِ إِنْ كُنْتُمْ إِيَّاهُ تَعْبُدُونَ

Believers! Eat the pure things that We have provided you, and be grateful to God alone if you worship only Him. (2:172)

قُلْ لَّا أَجِدُ فِي مَا أُوحِيَ إِلَيَّ مُحَرَّمًا عَلَى طَاعِمٍ يَّطْعَمُهُ إِلَّا أَنْ يَّكُونَ مَيْتَةً أَوْ دَمًا مَّسْفُوحًا أَوْ لَحْمَ

خِنْزِيرٍ فَإِنَّهُ رِجْسٌ أَوْ فِسْقًا أُهِلَّ لِغَيْرِ اللهِ بِهِ

Tell them [O Messenger]: I find not in what has been revealed to me through inspiration forbidden to a person who eats edible things, unless it be carrion, or blood poured forth, or the flesh of swine, because these are unclean or, in disobedience to God, animals slaughtered in someone else's name. (6:145)

- In some Ahadith, the Prophet is reported to have prohibited the consumption of meat from beasts with sharp canine teeth, birds with claws and tentacles in their feet, and tamed donkeys.

- Upon examining the Quranic verses, it becomes clear that these statements merely delineate the innate guidance inherent in human nature, rather than providing new instructions.

- We all know naturally that lions, tigers, elephants, eagles, crows, vultures, snakes, scorpions, and human flesh are not meant for consumption.

- If paying attention to the words of God, we can easily conclude that God does not have to list edible things in the Quran.

- What the Quran lists are those things that people could mistakenly eat due to a difference of opinion about them.

8. Role of Previous Scriptures in Understanding the Quran

وَأَنزَلْنَا إِلَيْكَ الْكِتَابَ بِالْحَقِّ مُصَدِّقًا لِّمَا بَيْنَ يَدَيْهِ مِنَ الْكِتَابِ **وَمُهَيْمِنًا** عَلَيْهِ فَاحْكُم بَيْنَهُم بِمَا أَنزَلَ اللَّهُ وَلاَ تَتَّبِعْ أَهْوَاءَهُمْ عَمَّا جَاءَكَ مِنَ الْحَقِّ

And [O Prophet!] We have revealed the Book with the truth in confirmation of it before it, and standing as **a Guardian over it.** Therefore, give judgment among men according to the guidance revealed by God and do not yield to their whims by swerving from the truth revealed to you. (5:48)

- In this verse, the Quran is regarded as a guardian over previous scriptures. In light of its own description (scale, criterion, guardian), one can conclude:
  - The Quran is the only authentic and trustworthy version of the Book of God now on the face of the earth.
  - Since the texts of other scriptures were lost to posterity and their translations were extensively tampered with, it is this Quran that is preserved to judge between the right and wrong of those scriptures now.
  - Whatever it declares to be right is right, and whatever it declares to be wrong is wrong and must necessarily be rejected.
  - Everyone must turn to it only to resolve differences of opinion.
  - Nothing can be a judge on it; it shall reign supreme in the dominion of religion, and every person is bound not to make it subservient to any other thing.
- It is important to note that the books of the Bible are more in the nature of historical records and memoirs compiled by human authors decades or centuries after the prophets' times, rather than the verbatim words of God, which impacts their overall reliability compared to the Quran.
- When the Quran touches on a shared historical event, the Bible can sometimes provide additional context or details, provided they do not contradict the Quran's clear message or established facts.

9. Significance of Alif-Laam

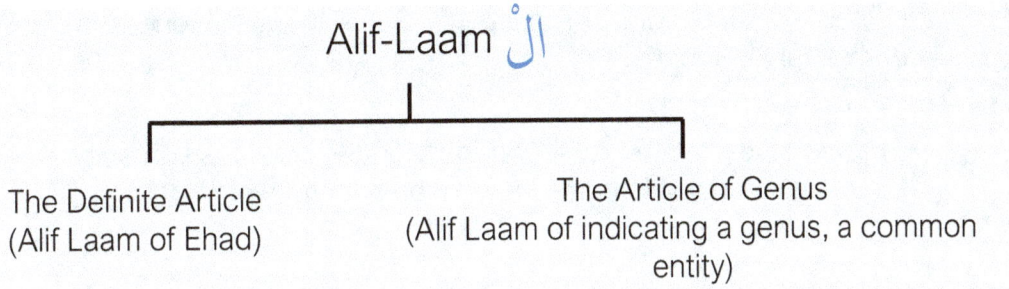

Alif-Laam ٱل

The Definite Article
(Alif Laam of Ehad)

The Article of Genus
(Alif Laam of indicating a genus, a common entity)

- Alif-Laam is used for different purposes but the Alif-Laam that is significant for our discussion is called "*Alif Laam Harfi*" (ال حرفى).

- It is a particle that comes at the beginning of a noun and renders the noun definite. It is the equivalent of the word "the" in English. It normally functions as a definite article and has many uses in Arabic.

- In the Arabic language, the article Alif Laam serves as both a definite article (denoting something specific to a time and place) and an indicator of a common entity (such as a family of something) without specifying (for example, the man may refer to human beings, depending on the context).

- There is a very specific use of Alif-Laam before the noun when something is already mentioned or in the minds of the author and the readers; an Alif-Laam is used before that. For example, in English, when we say, "I bought a pen. The pen is very good". Here, "the" before the pen goes back to the pen that I mentioned in the previous sentence.

- This is exactly how it works in the Quran. When the Quran uses terms like Al-Mushrikun, Al-Yahud, and Al-Nasara, it refers to specific groups of people living in the time and place the Quran addresses, not to every idolator, Jew, or Christian in the world.

- They were the direct addressees of the Quran; any instruction regarding them cannot be extended to those living around us.

- In most cases, it is the context, related factors, and natural indicators that help a serious student of the Quran distinguish between these two types of Alif Laam.

10. Parentheses in the Quran

- There are many places in the Quran where a comment is inserted (text in parentheses without actual brackets) by God – these sentences are called Parenthetical Sentences.
- There are two types:
  - Parenthetical sentences – comment on the previous sentence
  - Insertion – added to carry the conversation forward

Examples of Parenthetical Sentences

Then when she delivered the child, she said: "Lord, I have given birth to a daughter" – and God well knew of what she had delivered – and [said:] "That boy would not have been like this girl. And I have named her Mary, and I give her and her progeny in your refuge from Satan, the Accursed One." (3:36)

And if they break their oath after their pledge and find blame in your religion, wage war against these leaders of disbelief – their words and promises are baseless – so that they abstain. (9:12)

Recall when Luqman, while counselling his son, had said: "Son! Do not associate partners with God. In reality, polytheism is a great injustice – We have counselled a human being about his parents also. His mother kept him in her womb, tolerating woe after woe, and [after birth] it took two years for his weaning. [We have counselled him:] "Be grateful to Me and to your parents [and remember that ultimately] to Me is the return. But if they force you to associate someone with Me about whom you have no proof, do not obey them. However, treat them kindly in this world and follow the way of those who turn to Me. Then you will have to return to Me alone. Then I shall inform you of what you have been doing." – Son! The fact is that if a deed is equal to even the grain of a mustard seed …… (31:13-15)

> As a parent, Luqman did not consider it right to discuss his rights and the sacrifices that parents make, so God inserted this into his talk.

Assignment

Write the meaning of the following Quranic Words as they are used in the Quran in different verses:

تَذْلِيلًا   غَلِيظٌ   الْكِتَابَ   الْجَاهِلُ   الْخَبِيثُ   زَوْجٍ   زَكَّىٰ

شَجَرَ   غُلْفٌ   شَرَابٌ   حِجَابٌ   الْقُلُوبُ   الْحَمْدُ   الزَّكَاة

الْحُوتُ   الْمَسْكَنَةُ   السَّبُعُ   طَبَعَ   شَدِيدٌ   مَقْبُوضَةٌ   ضَرَبَ

لَبِسٍ   لِبَاسٌ   غَبَرَةٌ   ذِكْرٌ   الذَّكَرُ   شَأْنٍ   أُمَّةً

https://corpus.quran.com/

Chapter 13

Collection and Transmission of the Quran

In this chapter, we will discuss the collection of the Quran at the time of Prophet Muhammad and in later periods.

The piecemeal revelation of the Quran

- The Quran was not revealed to Prophet Muhammad as a complete book.
- The Quran was revealed over more than two decades (around 23 years), according to the needs and circumstances of the Prophet and his companions.
- It was revealed in a different sequence/order, but compiled in a completely different one.
- According to the Quran, it was already written by God on a Safe and Secure Tablet (Loh-e-Mahfooz) before it was revealed to Prophet Muhammad via Angel Jibrael.
- Finally, when it was gathered and arranged in a new sequence (which could be the same as it was in Loh-e-Mahfooz), the Prophet was asked to follow this final arrangement.
- The Quran is with us now in that final order.

The wisdom behind piecemeal revelation

- The most compelling evidence that God is with the Prophet, seeing and hearing everything.
- The Quran was revealed in response to the situation the Prophet faced, providing him with support and assurance.
- A complete book will lose its significance and relevance in the mission of the Prophet.
- It would have overwhelmed a society that had deviated from the Sunnah of Prophet Ibrahim.
- Temporary instructions can be given and then removed in the final version.
- It became easy for people to memorize it.

- The Quran also mentions the wisdom behind it.

وَ قُرْاٰنًا فَرَقْنٰهُ لِتَقْرَاَهٗ عَلَى النَّاسِ عَلٰى مُكْثٍ وَّ نَزَّلْنٰهُ تَنْزِيْلًا

And We have revealed this Quran in portions so that you can recite it to people slowly but surely, and precisely for this purpose, We have revealed it with due diligence. (Bani-Israel 106)

وَ قَالَ الَّذِيْنَ كَفَرُوْا لَوْ لَا نُزِّلَ عَلَيْهِ الْقُرْاٰنُ جُمْلَةً وَّاحِدَةً كَذٰلِكَ لِنُثَبِّتَ بِهٖ فُؤَادَكَ وَ رَتَّلْنٰهُ تَرْتِيْلًا

These disbelievers say: "Why was this Quran not revealed to him completely at one time?" We have done this so that We can strengthen your heart through this, and that's why We have read this to you slowly and gradually. (Furqan 32)

Revelation Process

- The Quran does not describe the entire step-by-step process, but various passages make it clear that this is the process of revelation and that the Surahs of the Quran are organized accordingly at different stages of revelation.

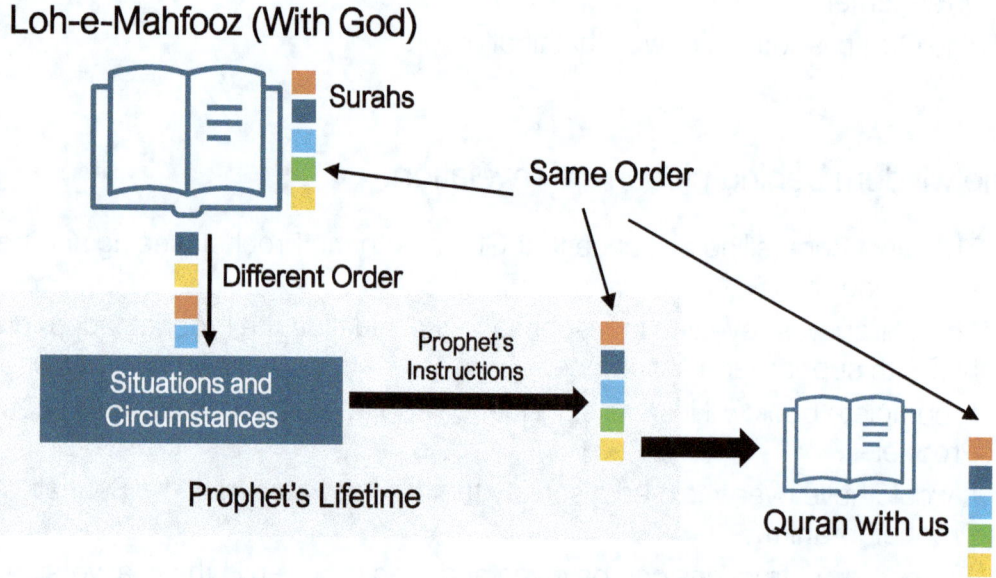

- The Quran mentioned how it all started and where the Quran originally was.

بَلْ هُوَ قُرْآنٌ مَّجِيدٌ ۙ فِى لَوْحٍ مَّحْفُوظٍ

In fact, this is the exalted Quran. It is in the Preserved Tablet.
(Buruj 21-22)

إِنَّهُ لَقُرْآنٌ كَرِيمٌ ۙ فِى كِتَابٍ مَّكْنُونٍ

Undoubtedly, this is a glorious Quran in a protected book.
(Waqiah 77-78)

كَلَّا إِنَّهَا تَذْكِرَةٌ ۖ فَمَن شَآءَ ذَكَرَهُ ۙ فِى صُحُفٍ مُّكَرَّمَةٍ

Certainly not! This is just a reminder. So, whoever wishes can be reminded
through it, written in honorable Tablets (Abasa 11-13)

- The picture on the previous page shows one of the ways the Quran is revealed from
  its origin (with God) to our hands. It is one of the possibilities among many when it
  comes to the order of the Surahs.
- According to the Quran, it was already written by God in the same sequence as we
  have it today (the Quran is silent on this matter).
- God revealed the Quran from the Loh-e-Mahfooz to the heart of Prophet
  Muhammad in a completely different order, as per the situation of the Prophet.
- Prophet Muhammad instructed the scribes to write it down and memorize it in the
  same order as we have it today.
- This suggests that the order of the Surah in the Loh-e-Mahfooz and what we have
  today in the Mushaf is the same.
- This is apparent from the Quran's statement in Surah Waqiah (see above):
  "undoubtedly, this is a glorious Quran in a protected book."

Protection at the time of Revelation

- The word *Loh-e-Mahfooz* means "The Protected Tablet."
- The Qur'an mentions it to reassure Prophet Muhammad and his people that this Book is under God's special protection. It is not a human work, nor something whispered by Satan. It is a divine revelation, safeguarded at every stage.
  - From the beginning, the Qur'an was in *Loh-e-Mahfooz*.
  - God sent it down through His most powerful and trusted angel, Jibreel.
  - God placed it firmly in the heart of Prophet Muhammad, ensuring it was received exactly as it was revealed.
- The Quran says: "No falsehood can approach it from the front or the back." This means neither Satan nor any other being can add, remove, or distort anything in it.
- The Quraysh claimed that the Quran was only thoughts suggested by Satan into the Prophet's heart (called *ilqaa*).
- The Qur'an recounts a time when the jinn attempted to listen to the heavenly words by hiding in the skies. They found that the skies were now guarded, and whenever they tried to eavesdrop, meteors chased them away. This shows that divine revelation was being specially protected.
- We do not know all the details of how the Qur'an exists in Loh-e-Mahfooz. But based on the Qur'an's words, there is no reason to think it is any different.

In fact, <u>this</u> is the exalted Quran. It is in the Preserved Tablet. (Buruj 21-22)

God's scheme for protecting the Quran after the revelation

- In the Quran, God had already informed the Prophet that He would protect it so it could be delivered to humanity both during his lifetime and afterward.
- It was critical because Prophet Muhammad was the last prophet, and the practice of revelation would cease with him
- God revealed this scheme to Prophet Muhammad during the revelation of the Quran.

God's Promise

إِنَّا نَحْنُ نَزَّلْنَا الذِّكْرَ وَ إِنَّا لَهُ لَحْفِظُونَ

We have sent down this reminder, and only We shall protect it. (Hijr:9)

God's Scheme

لَا تُحَرِّکْ بِهِ لِسَانَکَ لِتَعْجَلَ بِهِ

إِنَّ عَلَيْنَا جَمْعَهُ وَ قُرْآنَهُ

فَإِذَا قَرَأْنَاهُ فَاتَّبِعْ قُرْآنَهُ ثُمَّ إِنَّ عَلَيْنَا بَيَانَهُ

Don't move your tongue in haste to get it all, its collection and recitation (final recitation) is upon Us, and when we have recited it to you, follow its recitation. Then its explanation is upon Us (Qiyamah:16-19)

- God revealed the scheme and gave the following instructions to the Prophet:
    - Be assured, He will protect the Quran.
    - There is no need to worry about quickly memorizing the Quran out of fear of loss when it is revealed – God will collect and protect it.
    - It is upon God to re-arrange and collect the Quran in its final form in the lifetime of the Prophet, and the Prophet will not forget any of it.
    - The **second/final recital** would take place in this new sequence once the Quran has been arranged as a Book.
    - The Prophet is then **bound to follow this new order** and recital of the Quran.
    - God will also explain anything that requires explanation in the lifetime of the Prophet.

Final Recital of the Quran

سَنُقْرِئُكَ فَلَا تَنْسَى ۚ إِلَّا مَا شَاءَ اللهُ

(Similarly, the Quran will also reach its culmination one day, and then soon) We will recite it to you, then you will not forget except what Allah pleases (Surah Aala:6-7)

- The verses of Surah Qiyamah, Aala, and some other Surahs clearly indicate that God promised to collect the Quran during the Prophet's lifetime, and that before the Prophet's death, it was presented to him in its final form.
- This final recital (after the collection) is also termed Al Ardah Al Akhirah (the Final Presentation).
- Besides the Quran, many Ahadith also record the compilation and final recital of the Quran in the lifetime of the Prophet – the Prophet had assigned many Scribes of the Quran who used to write the Quran as per the instruction of the Prophet.

Abu Huraira reported: Jibrael used to repeat the recitation of the Quran with the Prophet once a year, but he repeated it twice with him in the year he died … (Sahih Bukhari #4998) (some reports suggested that it happened in the last two years)

Fatimah reported: The Prophet said, "Jibrael would come to me to revise the Quran once every year. This year, he revised with me twice. I do not think it means anything but that my life will end. Verily, you will be the first of the people of my house to meet me." (Sahih Bukhari #3376)

Collection and Compilation of the Quran in the Prophet's lifetime

- Islamic scholarship on the compilation of the Quran typically focuses on the period of Caliph Uthman, during which the criteria for determining what the Quran is and what it is not were standardized. This was needed because new Muslims were reading different interpretations of the Quran that had been allowed during the initial period of revelation, before the final recital.

- However, many scholars of the Quran's history have concluded that the entire Quran was collected and compiled in a single book form during the lifetime of Prophet Muhammad.

- Some earlier historical reports also suggest that it is quite reasonable to think that if the Quran had been collected (memorized and written) entirely under divine guidance, the Prophet would have compiled it into a complete book in his lifetime.

Zayd has reported saying: "We used to compile the Quran from small scraps in the presence of the Messenger." (Hakim, Mustadrak)

Malik said that no one should carry the Mushaf by its strap, nor on a pillow unless he is clean… (Muwatta, Kitab Al-Nida Lil-Salah)

Qatadah said: I asked Anas Ibn Malik: 'Who collected the Quran at the time of the Prophet?' He replied: 'Four, all of whom were from the Ansar: Ubay Ibn Kaab, Muadh Ibn Jabal, Zayd Ibn Thabit, and Abu Zayd.' (Sahih Bukhari #5003)

Malik reported that the Prophet said: "I have left you with two matters which will never lead you astray, as long as you hold to them: the Book of Allah and the Sunnah of His Prophet." (Al Muwatta #1661)

Abu Abd al-Rahman al Sulaimi reports, "The reading of Abu Bakr, Umar, Uthman, Zayd ibn Thabit, and that of all the Muhajirun and the Ansar was the same. They read the Quran using the Qira'at al Ammah (Common Recital). This is the same reading that the Prophet read out twice to Jibrael in the year of his death. Zayd ibn Thabit was also present in this reading [called] the "Ardah-I akhirah." It was this very reading that he taught the Quran to people till his death". (Al Zarkashi Al Burhan fi Ulum Al Quran p237)

The concept of consensus and perpetuity

- Let's understand these important concepts with an example, as they help ascertain the authenticity of the Quran.
- During WWII, many people witnessed it firsthand, while others heard about it.

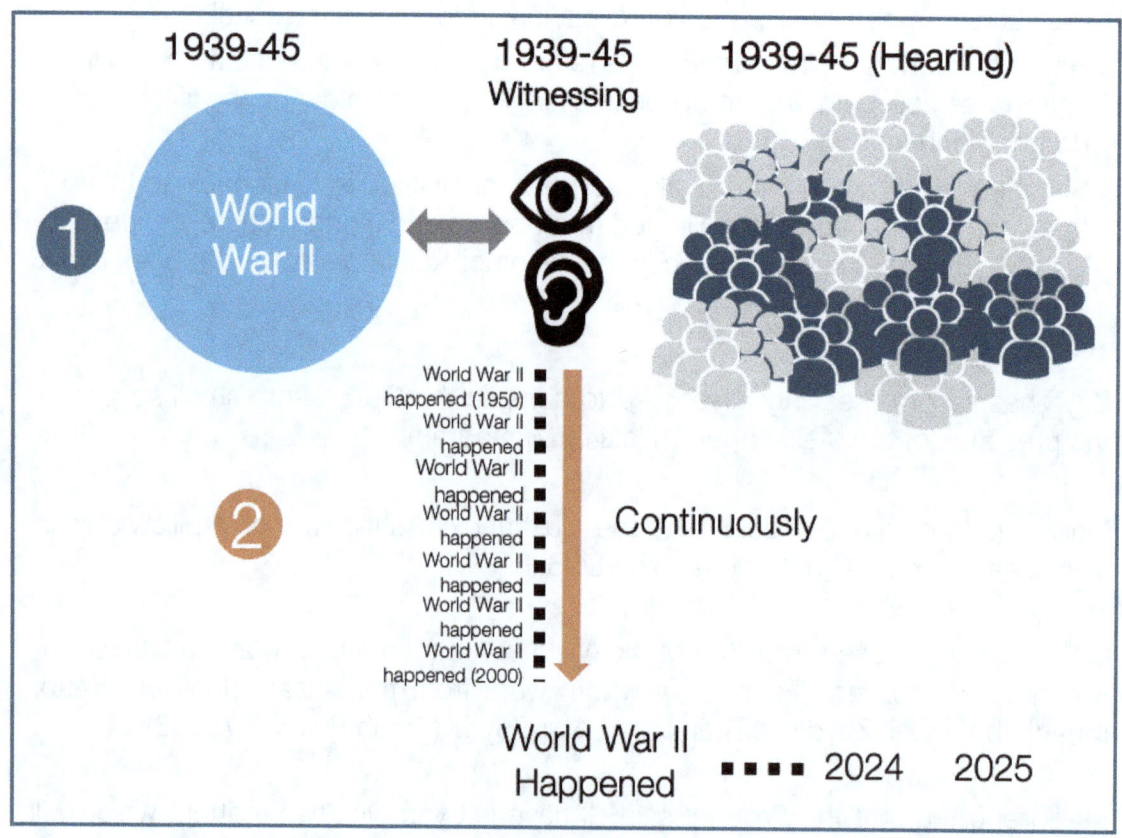

1 Consensus

So many people are witnessing and hearing about it firsthand at different places that it is hard to believe that they are all lying about its occurrence

2 Perpetuity

Today, we still hear about it with no break or gap in transmitting something from the time it started up until today

The method of transmission of the Quran

- The Quran, with the new arrangement (Text) and final recital (Reading), was transmitted to future generations by the companions of the Prophet
- It canceled all readings (or texts) of the chronological version of the Quran
- The companions transmitted the new order and the final recital to the next generation through their consensus (Ijma) and perpetual concurrence (Tawatur) – it has been a never-ending effort since that time

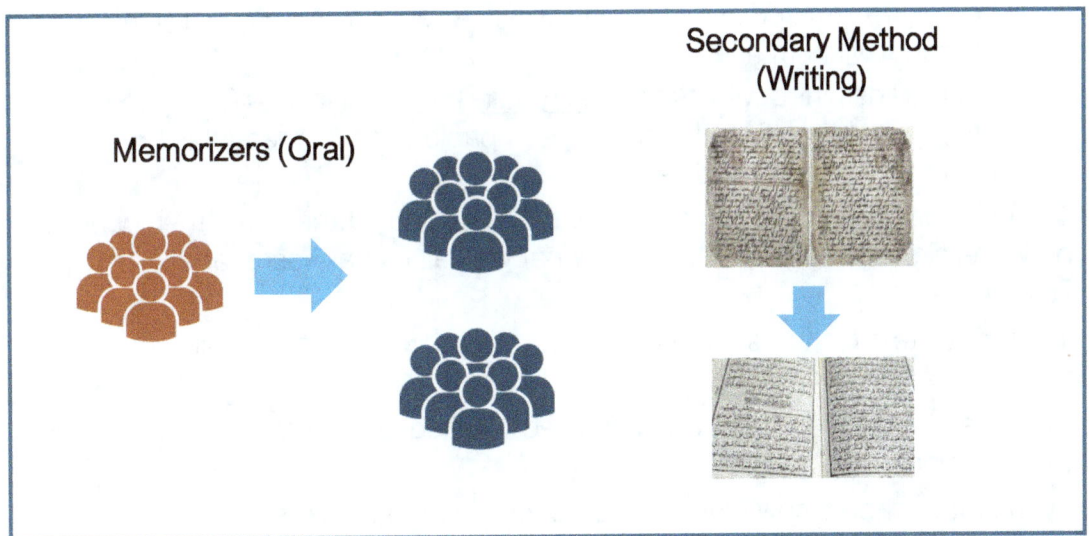

Consensus (Ijma)

Each companion vouched that the large number of copies being transmitted is, in fact, the same Quran revealed to Prophet Muhammad. This is the Quran they have heard and read throughout their lives, and none of them deviates from its final text. This consensus has existed in every generation of Muslims

Perpetuity (Tawatur)

A large number of people relay information from the senses at every stage, making collusion on falsehood almost impossible. The number of sources is replicated and multiplied many times at every step. One generation passed on to the next. This has been going on for the last 14 centuries now without a gap

Transmission of Qiraat Al Ammah (Common/Popular Recital)

Only one recital was transmitted with consensus and perpetuity

- Although scholars of the Quran discuss multiple readings of the Quran, they all agree that the *"Qiraat al Aammah"* (the final and common recital) was the only recital transmitted through Oral and written Perpetuity (Tawatur) from generation to generation.
- The Quran is the **only** book in the world:
    - The **text** transmitted in its original form is what was written during the time of Prophet Muhammad.
    - That is transmitted with its **original reading or recital** also – God (the author) taught the Prophet and his companions how to read this book, and that was transferred as well.
- The companions had written copies of their own, but at that time, there were no vowel signs or sounds in the text (what we call Fatha, Kasra, and Dhamma).
- The written text (script) served as a supportive source, but the main source was oral transmission.
- All written text of the Quran was compiled, verified, and written based on oral transmission (memorization).
- Even today, when a new Quran is published, few memorizers verify it by reading it themselves before it is made available to the public.
- Two types of memorizers existed: a few memorized the complete Quran by the time of the death of Prophet Muhammad, while others memorized only partially. One group would memorize one set of Surahs, and another would memorize another.

Distribution of the Quran (with common recital) after Prophet Muhammad

- Within 10-15 years after Prophet Muhammad, Islam had spread far and wide, reaching Northwest Africa and Iran
- The new Muslims of these lands depended on Muslim armies and traders to learn about Islam and the Quran, but over time, it became difficult for people in these far lands to learn the Quran – most of the memorizers and the written scripts of the Quran were in Medinah.

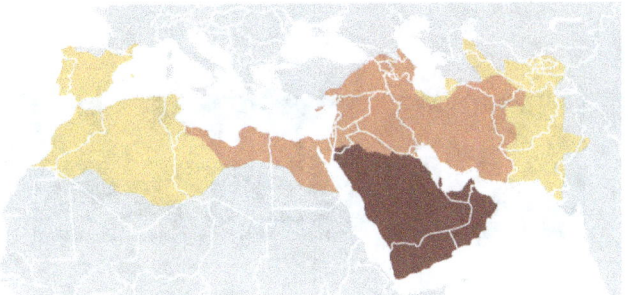

- Even the companions' copies of the Quran were not written in the final form and recited as discussed earlier.
- There were dialect differences among Arab tribes, and people tended to recite certain verses in their own dialects. The companions of the Prophet taught the Quran in these lands as they learned.
- This created a situation in which common people were confused about how to actually read a specific word or verse. In the time of Uthman, this problem was finally addressed.
- Through some of the renowned memorizers, he prepared multiple standard copies of the Quran from the original (Qiraat al Aammah) and sent them out to different lands
- Since that time, all Muslims have been reading that compilation.

There are multiple readings of the Quran that reach us through Ahadith. These are not like the Quran, which was transmitted to us through *Ijma* and *Tawatur*. Research and identify the names of those readings and the regions in which they are recited.

Chapter 14

Applying the Principles Examples

In this chapter, we will apply the principles we have learned in this course to various sections of the Quran and see how this approach makes a difference in our understanding.

Topics Covered

- This chapter covers the following topics we have learned, along with the specific Quranic passages related to them.

  - ❖ Importance of the Context in the Quran
  - ❖ Similes & Metaphors Used in the Quran
  - ❖ Sudden Shifts in Addressees
  - ❖ Shifting to the Indirect Address
  - ❖ Parenthetical Sentences
  - ❖ Insertion in the Middle
  - ❖ Use of the Degrees in Verbs
  - ❖ Use of Alif-Laam
  - ❖ Oaths in the Quran
  - ❖ The Quran explains itself

- Most of the examples covered in this chapter are self-explanatory. However, for a more detailed explanation of the example verses covered, the following resources can be used:

  - **Al-Bayan** – the Quran Tafsir by Javed Ahmed Ghamidi

  https://www.javedahmadghamidi.com/quran-home (use English language)

  - **Tadabburul ul Quran** by Amin Ahsan Islahi

  https://amin-ahsan-islahi.org/english-books/

Examples of the Importance of the Context in the Quran

Surah Al-Ana'am Verse 38

مَا فَرَّطْنَا فِي الْكِتٰبِ مِنْ شَيْءٍ ثُمَّ اِلٰى رَبِّهِمْ يُحْشَرُوْنَ

We have left nothing out of this Book. After this, they will be gathered before their Lord. (Surah Anaam Verse 38)

- Without the context:

  - This verse alludes to Allah mentioning the details of every topic in the Quran.
  - Some classical interpreters of the Quran have taken this meaning.
  - **Conclusion:** The Quran has the solution for everything, directly or indirectly.

- Now, read the verse in its full context ….

If [despite this] you find their hatred hard to bear, see if you can find a trench in the earth or a stairway in the sky by which you may bring them a sign (to believe). Had God willed it, He could have guided them all so they would never become those overcome by emotion. Only those people shall accept [this call of Ours] who listen. As for these dead, [their fate now only is that] God will raise them; then they will be returned to Him. They say: "Why was no sign sent down to this prophet from his Lord?" Say: God can send down a sign [whenever He intends to], but most of them [make this demand because they] are unaware of its consequences. [Do you not see that] all the beasts that roam on their legs on the earth and all the birds that soar on both their wings in the air are all communities like your own. And [to make you understand] We have left nothing out of this Book (to make you know the facts related to God). After this, they will be gathered before their Lord. (Surah Anaam Verse 35-38)

Conclusion: When it comes to explaining the oneness of God and His Powers, nothing is left out in this book.

Surah Al-Anbiya Verse 92

إِنَّ هَٰذِهِ أُمَّتُكُمْ أُمَّةً وَّاحِدَةً

And this is your "ummah," and your "ummah" is one. (Surah Anbiya Verse 92)

Ummah = In the Arabic language, it means a group or community to which you belong

Without the context

- Prophet Muhammad belongs to a Muslim nation.
- The Muslim nation should live as one nation.
- It is against Allah's will to have separate Muslim countries.
- **Conclusion:** All Muslims should come under one Khilafah.

Now, read the verse in its full context ....

From Verse 48: Prophet Musa and his story are mentioned
From Verse 51: Prophet Ibrahim and his story are mentioned
From Verse 71: Prophet Lut and his story are mentioned
From Verse 76: Prophet Nuh and his story are mentioned
From Verse 78: Prophet Dawood, Suleiman, and their story are mentioned
From Verse 83: Prophet Ayyub and his story are mentioned
From Verse 85: Prophet Ismail, Idrees, and Dhul Kifl are mentioned
From Verse 87: Prophet Yunus and his story are mentioned
From Verse 89: Prophet Zakariah and his story are mentioned
From Verse 91: Prophet Jesus and his mother are mentioned
Finally, Verse 92: And this is your "ummah" and your "ummah" is one (in its message and their commitment to Allah)

Conclusion: All Messengers and Prophets brought the same message of Allah. Prophet Muhammad belongs to the same group, and he brought nothing different.

Surah An-Nisaa Verse 159

وَ اِنْ مِّنْ اَهْلِ الْكِتٰبِ اِلَّا لَيُؤْمِنَنَّ بِهٖ قَبْلَ مَوْتِهٖ ۚ وَ يَوْمَ الْقِيٰمَةِ يَكُوْنُ عَلَيْهِمْ شَهِيْدًا

Everyone from among these People of the Book shall definitely believe in him (Jesus) before his death, and on the Day of Judgement, he will bear witness to them. (4:159)

- Many translators and Mufassireen of the Quran have translated this verse as above without considering the full context of the preceding passage. The general understanding is:

  - The Jews have rejected Prophet Jesus (Isa), who was the final prophet sent to them among the Children of Israel.
  - The two verses before this one discussed Jesus, so this verse is also about him.
  - But before his physical death, everyone among the Jews (regardless of time and place) will ultimately believe in him.
  - And on the Day of Judgment, Jesus will be a witness over them.
  - **Conclusion:** Jesus will return in the end times, and all Jews will come to believe in Him (whether willingly or unwillingly).

- If the pronouns of "bi*hi*" and "moti*hi*" are referring to Jesus, then so many questions can be raised.
- If this is about Jesus' second coming, then many Jews have already died without believing in him. So, this statement cannot be true that every single Jew from the People of the Book will believe in him.
- Also, in many narrations about the second coming of Jesus, it is said that many Jews will be deceived by Dajjal, and Jesus will fight with them. This narration seems contrary to what this verse is telling us.

Surah An-Nisaa Verse 159

Now, read this verse in this entire context it came in:

Connect the two

These People of the Book ask you to bring down directly to them a book from the heavens [instead of this Quran]. So, this is no matter of wonder. Of Moses, they made an even greater demand. They had asked him: "Show us God face to face." Then, because of this rebelliousness, a thunderbolt struck them. After that, they deified the calf even when obvious signs had come to them; yet We still forgave this and had given Moses clear dominance [on them]. And We had lifted Tur over them with a covenant with them and had directed them: "Enter the gates [of the city] bowing your heads," and had said to them: "Do not be disobedient in the matter of the Sabbath," and [on all these things], We had taken from them a firm covenant. Then because they broke their covenant [We laid a curse on them] and because they denied the revelations of God and because they killed the prophets unjustly and because they said: "Our hearts have a covering on them." – no, in fact, it is God who has sealed their hearts because of their disbelief; so, [now] they will seldom embrace faith and because of their disbelief and because of their vicious accusation against Mary and because of their claim: "We have killed the Messiah, Jesus son of Mary, the Messenger of God." – even though neither did they kill him nor did they crucify him; in fact, the matter was muddled up for them. Those who disagree with this are afflicted with doubts about it; they have no knowledge about it; they are only following conjectures. They certainly did not slay him; in fact, God had lifted him up to Him. And God is Mighty, very Wise. [This is a list of their crimes; so, if they are now demanding that a book other than the Quran be directly revealed to them from the heavens, just ignore them. O Prophet!] Everyone from among these People of the Book shall definitely believe in [this Quran] before his death; and on the Day of Judgement it will bear witness to them.

- The people of the book asked Prophet Muhammad to bring down a book other than the Quran.
- God told Prophet Muhammad that there is nothing unusual about their behavior.
- God recounted all their crimes first.
- In the end, He told Prophet Muhammad that due to the victory that He will give to the Muslims and the punishment that will be meted out to the disbelievers, they will all recognize (here the belief is in the meaning of realizing, not believing from the heart) that this Book is the truth before they die in humiliation.

Examples of the Similes & Metaphors

Similes / Metaphors for Disbelievers

Surah Baqarah Verses 6-7 & 17-18

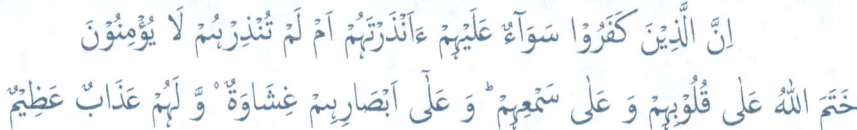

Their Behavior

اِنَّ الَّذِيۡنَ كَفَرُوۡا سَوَآءٌ عَلَيۡهِمۡ ءَاَنۡذَرۡتَهُمۡ اَمۡ لَمۡ تُنۡذِرۡهُمۡ لَا يُؤۡمِنُوۡنَ

خَتَمَ اللّٰهُ عَلٰى قُلُوۡبِهِمۡ وَ عَلٰى سَمۡعِهِمۡ ۚ وَ عَلٰۤى اَبۡصَارِهِمۡ غِشَاوَةٌ ۫ وَّ لَهُمۡ عَذَابٌ عَظِيۡمٌ

On the other hand, people who have decided to reject this Book, it is the same to them whether you warn them or not; they will not believe. God has now set a seal on their hearts and on their ears [per His law], and on their eyes is a veil, and [on the Day of Judgement] a great torment awaits them.

The Metaphor

مَثَلُهُمۡ كَمَثَلِ الَّذِى اسۡتَوۡقَدَ نَارًا ۚ فَلَمَّاۤ اَضَآءَتۡ مَا حَوۡلَهٗ ذَهَبَ اللّٰهُ

بِنُوۡرِهِمۡ وَ تَرَكَهُمۡ فِىۡ ظُلُمٰتٍ لَّا يُبۡصِرُوۡنَ صُمٌّ بُكۡمٌ عُمۡىٌ فَهُمۡ لَا يَرۡجِعُوۡنَ

Their example is like that of a person who kindled a large fire [in a dark night]; then, when the fire lit up the surroundings, God took away the ability to see for those for whom the fire had been kindled and left them in darkness, so that they could not see anything. Deaf, dumb, and blind; hence, they shall now never return.

- In the above example, the behavior of the rejectors and the consequences they faced are described metaphorically as people whose ability to see is taken away after someone (Prophet Muhammad) lit a fire, making the surroundings bright.
- In the next verse, God used another example of hypocrites, describing their behavior and consequences metaphorically as people walking in heavy rain with lightning. They walk a little, then wait when it gets too dark.

Similes / Metaphors for Hypocrites

Surah Baqarah Verses 8-10 & 19-20

Their Behavior

وَ مِنَ النَّاسِ مَنْ يَّقُوْلُ اٰمَنَّا بِاللّٰهِ وَ بِالْيَوْمِ الْاٰخِرِ وَ مَا هُمْ بِمُؤْمِنِيْنَ

يُخٰدِعُوْنَ اللّٰهَ وَ الَّذِيْنَ اٰمَنُوْا وَ مَا يَخْدَعُوْنَ اِلَّاۤ اَنْفُسَهُمْ وَ مَا يَشْعُرُوْنَ

فِيْ قُلُوْبِهِمْ مَّرَضٌ ۙ فَزَادَهُمُ اللّٰهُ مَرَضًا ۚ وَ لَهُمْ عَذَابٌ اَلِيْمٌۢ بِمَا كَانُوْا يَكْذِبُوْنَ

And among these people are those [Hypocrites] who say: "We have professed faith in God and in the Last Day," whereas they do not have faith in any of these things. They want to deceive both God and the believers, and in reality, they are only fooling themselves, but realize it not! In their hearts was the ailment [of jealousy]; so, God has now further increased this ailment of theirs. And because they have been lying, there is a grievous penalty for them.

The Metaphor

اَوْ كَصَيِّبٍ مِّنَ السَّمَآءِ فِيْهِ ظُلُمٰتٌ وَّ رَعْدٌ وَّ بَرْقٌ ۚ يَجْعَلُوْنَ اَصَابِعَهُمْ فِيْ

اٰذَانِهِمْ مِّنَ الصَّوَاعِقِ حَذَرَ الْمَوْتِ ؕ وَ اللّٰهُ مُحِيْطٌۢ بِالْكٰفِرِيْنَ

يَكَادُ الْبَرْقُ يَخْطَفُ اَبْصَارَهُمْ ؕ كُلَّمَاۤ اَضَآءَ لَهُمْ مَّشَوْا فِيْهِ ۙ وَ اِذَاۤ اَظْلَمَ عَلَيْهِمْ

قَامُوْا ؕ وَ لَوْ شَآءَ اللّٰهُ لَذَهَبَ بِسَمْعِهِمْ وَ اَبْصَارِهِمْ ؕ اِنَّ اللّٰهَ عَلٰى كُلِّ شَيْءٍ قَدِيْرٌ

Or is it such that it is raining; in it are dark clouds, and thunder and lightning also. They are trying to insert their fingers in their ears from the fear of death because of lightning, whereas God has encompassed such rejecters from all sides. The lightning snatches away their sight; when it lights up on them, they walk a little in it, and when darkness descends upon them, they stand still. If God willed, He could have also taken away their hearing and sight. Indeed, God has power over all things.

Monotheism vs Polytheism Parable

Surah Ibrahim Verses 24-26

The fruits of believing in one true God

اَلَمۡ تَرَ كَيۡفَ ضَرَبَ اللّٰهُ مَثَلًا كَلِمَةً طَيِّبَةً كَشَجَرَةٍ طَيِّبَةٍ اَصۡلُهَا ثَابِتٌ وَّ فَرۡعُهَا فِى السَّمَآءِ

تُؤۡتِىۤ اُكُلَهَا كُلَّ حِيۡنٍ بِاِذۡنِ رَبِّهَا ؕ وَ يَضۡرِبُ اللّٰهُ الۡاَمۡثَالَ لِلنَّاسِ لَعَلَّهُمۡ يَتَذَكَّرُوۡنَ

Have you not seen how God has mentioned the example of the noble word? It is like a noble tree whose roots are deep in the earth and whose branches are spread out in the air. It continues to bear fruit with the permission of its Lord in every season. [This is the example of the noble word.] And God cites parables for people so that they seek reminders

The evil of not believing in one true God

وَ مَثَلُ كَلِمَةٍ خَبِيۡثَةٍ كَشَجَرَةٍ خَبِيۡثَةٍ اجۡتُثَّتۡ مِنۡ فَوۡقِ الۡاَرۡضِ مَا لَهَا مِنۡ قَرَارٍ

And, in contrast to it, the example of the evil word is an evil tree that can be uprooted from above the earth; it has no stability.

- By comparing monotheism to a fruit-bearing tree, the Quran first makes evident that its roots are not only deeply and firmly implanted in human nature but also the most highly valued by God. In other words, the status it occupies in the heavens and earth is unparalleled.

- The second reality explained is that it derives nourishment and strength from both human nature and providence. This keeps it lush and luxurious at all times.

- On the other hand, there is a tree resembling wild foliage. It neither bears fruit nor flowers. No one can sit in its shade or obtain food from it. It has neither any basis in reason and human nature nor in the teachings of the prophets. It is like a wild bush that exists only on Earth's surface. It has no roots in the earth, nor is it spread high in the sky. The heavy winds of difficult circumstances can easily uproot it.

Examples of the Shift in Addressees

Multiple addressees
Shift in the addressee

Example 1 – Single Shift:

Wife of Al-Aziz   **Yusuf**

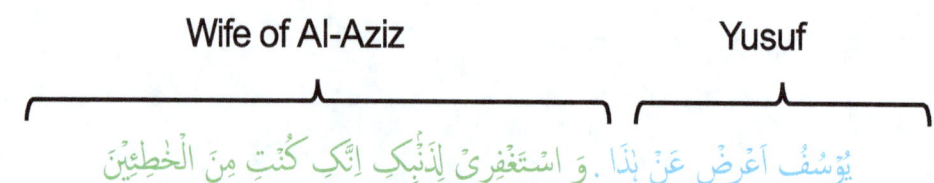

يُوسُفُ اَعْرِضْ عَنْ هٰذَا . وَ اسْتَغْفِرِىْ لِذَنْبِكِ اِنَّكِ كُنْتِ مِنَ الْخٰطِئِيْنَ

O Yusuf, let this matter go, (and O you woman!) Seek repentance for your sin because you are the actual wrongdoer. (Surah Yusuf:28)

- By using appropriate pronouns and verb forms, the Quran clearly indicates a shift in the addressee, and a reader of the Quran who is well-versed in Arabic cannot miss it.

Example 2 – Multiple Shifts:

Idolators   **Prophet Muhammad**

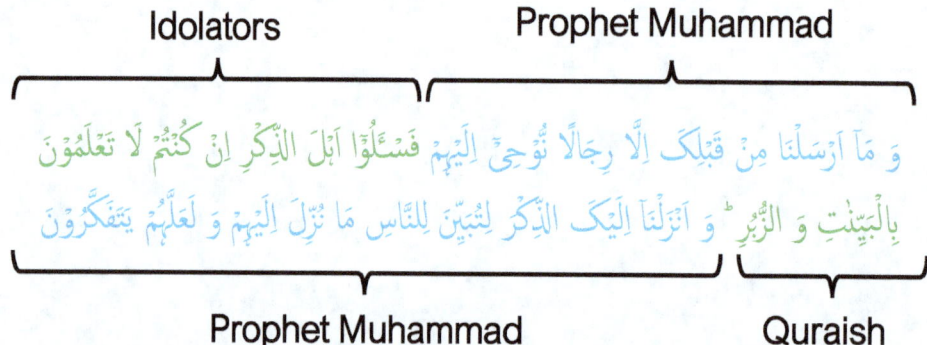

وَ مَا اَرْسَلْنَا مِنْ قَبْلِكَ اِلَّا رِجَالًا نُّوحِىْٓ اِلَيْهِمْ فَسْـَٔلُوْٓا اَهْلَ الذِّكْرِ اِنْ كُنْتُمْ لَا تَعْلَمُوْنَ

بِالْبَيِّنٰتِ وَ الزُّبُرِ ۗ وَ اَنْزَلْنَاۤ اِلَيْكَ الذِّكْرَ لِتُبَيِّنَ لِلنَّاسِ مَا نُزِّلَ اِلَيْهِمْ وَ لَعَلَّهُمْ يَتَفَكَّرُوْنَ

Prophet Muhammad   **Quraish**

[They insist that angels be sent down to them.] In reality, before you, too, We had sent men as messengers to whom We would send revelations. So, if you people do not know, ask those who [before this] received the reminder. We had sent them with proofs and Books. And now, We have revealed this reminder to you so that you may mention to these people what has been revealed to them and so that they may reflect. (Surah Nahl: 43-44)

- The above verse began by addressing the Prophet Muhammad, but then shifted to the Quraish and the People of the Book because of their objection. The address then returned to Prophet Muhammad, where it began.

Shift from indirect to direct address (Multiple Reasons)

- As in other languages, the shift from indirect to direct address, or vice versa, occurs for many reasons, especially when an orator is addressing a large crowd that comprises multiple groups.

Example 1

Indirect Address ⟶ وَ كُلَّ اِنْسَانٍ اَلْزَمْنٰهُ طَٰٓئِرَهٗ فِىْ عُنُقِهٖ ۚ وَ نُخْرِجُ لَهٗ يَوْمَ الْقِيٰمَةِ كِتٰبًا يَّلْقٰهُ مَنْشُوْرًا

Direct Address ⟶ اِقْرَأْ كِتٰبَكَ ۚ كَفٰى بِنَفْسِكَ الْيَوْمَ عَلَيْكَ حَسِيْبًا

[By relying on their deities, they should not hastily demand the torment.] We have tied each person's fate with his neck, and on the Day of Judgement, We shall bring forth a register for him which he will find open right before him. Here it is. "Read your account of deeds. Today, you yourself are sufficient to take your own account."   (Bani Israel 13-14)

> **Reason:** One reason the Quran shifts from indirect to direct is to emphasize a fact by presenting it before the addressees' eyes. We do it all the time in our language. A speaker may be talking in the 3rd person but suddenly shift to the 2nd person to warn the people.

Example 2

وَ قَالُوا اتَّخَذَ الرَّحْمٰنُ وَلَدًا   لَقَدْ جِئْتُمْ شَيْئًا اِدًّا

تَكَادُ السَّمٰوٰتُ يَتَفَطَّرْنَ مِنْهُ وَ تَنْشَقُّ الْاَرْضُ وَ تَخِرُّ الْجِبَالُ هَدًّا

اَنْ دَعَوْا لِلرَّحْمٰنِ وَلَدًا وَ مَا يَنْبَغِىْ لِلرَّحْمٰنِ اَنْ يَّتَّخِذَ وَلَدًا

They say: "The Merciful God has children." Very grave is this statement you have given. It may well be that because of this, the heavens tear apart, the earth is rent asunder, and the mountains collapse to fall down, that people have ascribed children to the Merciful God. It is not befitting for the Merciful to make anyone His children.
(Maryam 88-92)

> **Reason:** Another reason the Quran shifts from indirect to direct is when it wants to show Allah's wrath and anger targeted toward specific people. Allah SWT wanted to tell the Christians by addressing them directly that they had said something horrible.

Shift from indirect to direct address (Multiple Reasons)

Example 3

اِنَّ الْمُتَّقِيْنَ فِيْ جَنّٰتٍ وَّ نَعِيْمٍ ۙ فٰكِهِيْنَ بِمَآ اٰتٰىهُمْ رَبُّهُمْ ۚ وَ وَقٰىهُمْ رَبُّهُمْ عَذَابَ الْجَحِيْمِ

كُلُوْا وَ اشْرَبُوْا هَنِيْئًۢا بِمَا كُنْتُمْ تَعْمَلُوْنَ

The righteous, however, will be in gardens and bliss, enjoying what their Lord has blessed them with and that their Lord has preserved them from the torment of Hell. Now eat and drink with relish as a reward for the deeds you have been doing. (Tur 17-19)

> **Reason:** Another reason the Quran shifts from indirect to direct is to show honor and respect for the people who are rewarded on the Day of Judgment.

Example 4

اَلْحَمْدُ لِلّٰهِ رَبِّ الْعٰلَمِيْنَ ۙ الرَّحْمٰنِ الرَّحِيْمِ ۙ مٰلِكِ يَوْمِ الدِّيْنِ ۚ

اِيَّاكَ نَعْبُدُ وَ اِيَّاكَ نَسْتَعِيْنُ ۚ

Gratitude is for God only, the Lord of the universe, the Most Gracious, the Ever-Merciful, Who is the Master of the Day of Judgement. You alone we worship and only Your help we seek. (Surah Fatiha 1-4)

> **Reason:** Surah Fatiha is a dua, and God taught us how to make dua and ask for help. All the praises were in the third person, but suddenly the request was presented in the first person to show love and closeness to God and the person's dedication to Him alone.

Example 5

بَرَآءَةٌ مِّنَ اللهِ وَ رَسُوْلِهٖۤ اِلَى الَّذِيْنَ عٰهَدْتُّمْ مِّنَ الْمُشْرِكِيْنَ

فَسِيْحُوْا فِى الْاَرْضِ اَرْبَعَةَ اَشْهُرٍ وَّ اعْلَمُوْۤا اَنَّكُمْ غَيْرُ مُعْجِزِى اللهِ ۙ وَ اَنَّ اللهَ مُخْزِى الْكٰفِرِيْنَ

A declaration of acquittal is made by God and His Messenger for the Idolaters with whom you had made agreements. So, [O Idolaters of Arabia!] walk about now in the land for four more months and know that you cannot defeat God and that God shall certainly humiliate those who deny [His prophet].

> **Reason:** A general announcement has been made stating that after a few months, the disbelievers will be punished by death. In the middle, God turned towards the disbelievers and delivered the warning to them.

Examples of shifting to the Indirect Address

Indirectly addressing opponents through the Prophet

Example 1

- In these verses, God is stating the fact to Prophet Muhammad that, similar to Mushrikeen, the Jews and the Christians will not follow him until he follows them.
- They are not interested in making efforts to understand the Truth, which, according to God, should be the criterion for guidance.
- God is addressing the Prophet (indirectly to Muslims also), but the language suggests the real addressees are his opponents. No one would expect that the Prophet would surrender to his desires.

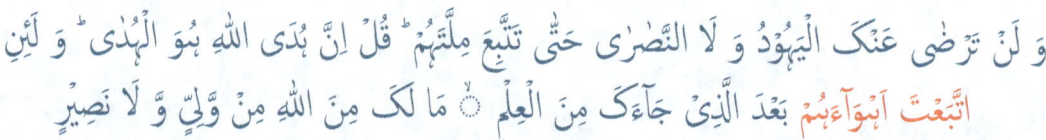

These Jews and Christians shall never be pleased with you unless you adopt their faith. [Therefore,] say: God's guidance is the only real guidance, and [you should know that] if, after the knowledge that has come to you, you yield to their desires, you will not have any friend against God or anyone to help you.
(Baqarah 120)

Example 2

- God is addressing the Prophet, but the language suggests the addressees are Muslims in general. The reason is that the instructions apply to all Muslims, not just the Prophet Muhammad.

يَا أَيُّهَا النَّبِيُّ إِذَا طَلَّقْتُمُ النِّسَاءَ فَطَلِّقُوهُنَّ لِعِدَّتِهِنَّ وَ أَحْصُوا الْعِدَّةَ

O Prophet! When you people divorce your wives, divorce them according to their waiting period and properly count the waiting period (Talaq 1)

Examples of the Parenthetical Sentences

Parenthetical Sentences

Example 1

فَلَمَّا وَضَعَتْهَا قَالَتْ رَبِّ اِنِّى وَضَعْتُهَآ اُنْثَى ۗ وَ اللّٰهُ اَعْلَمُ بِمَا وَضَعَتْ ۗ وَ لَيْسَ الذَّكَرُ كَالْاُنْثَى ۗ وَ اِنِّى سَمَّيْتُهَا مَرْيَمَ وَ اِنِّى اُعِيْذُهَا بِكَ وَ ذُرِّيَّتَهَا مِنَ الشَّيْطٰنِ الرَّجِيْمِ

Then when she delivered the child, she said: "Lord, I have given birth to a daughter" – <u>and God well knew what she had delivered</u> – and [said:] "That boy would not have been like this girl. [Well! This is what I have now] and I have named her Mary and I give her and her progeny in your refuge from Satan, the Accursed One." (Surah Aal-e-Imran:36)

- God says that although Maryam's mother is surprised, it was not a surprise to God. Even when her mother made dua, He already knew that Maryam's mother would deliver a baby girl. The best way to read this is to skip the parenthetical sentence and reread the complete verse without it.

Example 2

وَ اِنْ نَّكَثُوٓا اَيْمَانَهُمْ مِّنْ بَعْدِ عَهْدِهِمْ وَ طَعَنُوْا فِىْ دِيْنِكُمْ فَقَاتِلُوٓا اَئِمَّةَ الْكُفْرِ ۙ اِنَّهُمْ لَآ اَيْمَانَ لَهُمْ لَعَلَّهُمْ يَنْتَهُوْنَ

And if even after this treaty they have made, they go back on their word (betray) and find blame in your religion, then fight also these leaders of disbelief. <u>Their words and promises are baseless.</u> [Soon or late, they will break their promise;] hence, fight them so that they abstain from disbelief and polytheism. (Surah Tawbah:12)

- God is again commenting that He has asked Muslims to fight these leaders, and He knew they would break their contract because they were not serious about doing it. At the time they were doing it, God knew that their words and promises were baseless (they were liars) and that they would not abide by them. So, now fight with them.

Examples of the Insertion in the Middle

Insertion in the middle to complete the topic

وَ لَقَدْ اٰتَيْنَا لُقْمٰنَ الْحِكْمَةَ اَنِ اشْكُرْ لِلّٰهِ ۚ وَ مَنْ يَّشْكُرْ فَاِنَّمَا يَشْكُرُ لِنَفْسِهٖ ۚ وَ مَنْ كَفَرَ فَاِنَّ اللّٰهَ غَنِيٌّ حَمِيْدٌ

وَ اِذْ قَالَ لُقْمٰنُ لِابْنِهٖ وَ هُوَ يَعِظُهٗ يٰبُنَيَّ لَا تُشْرِكْ بِاللّٰهِ ۚ اِنَّ الشِّرْكَ لَظُلْمٌ عَظِيْمٌ

وَ وَصَّيْنَا الْاِنْسَانَ بِوَالِدَيْهِ ۚ حَمَلَتْهُ اُمُّهٗ وَهْنًا عَلٰى وَهْنٍ وَّ فِصٰلُهٗ فِيْ عَامَيْنِ اَنِ اشْكُرْ لِيْ وَ لِوَالِدَيْكَ ۚ اِلَيَّ الْمَصِيْرُ

وَ اِنْ جَاهَدٰكَ عَلٰۤى اَنْ تُشْرِكَ بِيْ مَا لَيْسَ لَكَ بِهٖ عِلْمٌ ۙ فَلَا تُطِعْهُمَا وَ صَاحِبْهُمَا فِى الدُّنْيَا

مَعْرُوْفًا ۖ وَّ اتَّبِعْ سَبِيْلَ مَنْ اَنَابَ اِلَيَّ ۚ ثُمَّ اِلَيَّ مَرْجِعُكُمْ فَاُنَبِّئُكُمْ بِمَا كُنْتُمْ تَعْمَلُوْنَ

يٰبُنَيَّ اِنَّهَآ اِنْ تَكُ مِثْقَالَ ...

حَبَّةٍ

We also gave this wisdom to Luqman and directed: "Be grateful to God" – and he who is grateful will be grateful for himself, and he who is ungrateful, God does not care about him because God is self-sufficient; He has praiseworthy attributes. Recall when Luqman, while counseling his son, had said: "Son! Do not associate partners with God. In reality, polytheism is a great injustice." [There is no doubt that] We have also counseled a human being about his parents. His mother kept him in her womb, tolerating distress after distress, and [after birth] it took two years for his weaning. [We have counseled him:] "Be grateful to Me and to your parents [and remember that ultimately] to Me is the return. But if they force you to associate someone with Me about whom you have no proof, do not obey them. However, treat them kindly in this world and follow the way of those who turn to Me. Then you will have to return to Me alone. Then I shall inform you of what you have been doing." [Luqman had said:] "Son! The fact is that if a deed is equal to even the grain ...... (Surah Luqman: 12-16)

- Green – Allah inserted this entire section to complete the topic and the message that He wanted to convey.
- In many places in the Quran, Allah reminds people of the rights of parents right after His rights.
- In this conversation, Luqman talked about Allah's right to be worshipped alone, but he felt shy about talking about his own rights, being a parent himself.
- Allah inserted these verses in the middle as He wanted to reemphasize the rights of parents for two reasons:
  - Honor Luqman, as he skipped advising his son on his own rights
  - Complete the topic of great advice given by a great wise man
- When we read the inserted verses, it is clear that they cannot be Luqman's statement.

Examples of the Use of the Degrees in Verbs

Degrees in Verbs

- Verbs in every language have various degrees and levels of the action that they describe.
- A verb may represent:
  - Decision of that action
  - The intention of that action
  - The Result of that action
  - Permanence of that action
  - Completeness of that action

Decision

إِنَّ الَّذِينَ **كَفَرُوا** سَوَآءٌ عَلَيْهِمْ ءَأَنذَرْتَهُمْ أَمْ لَمْ تُنذِرْهُمْ لَا يُؤْمِنُونَ

On the other hand, it is the same for those <u>who have decided to reject</u> this Book. Whether you warn them or not, they will not believe you. (2:6)

إِنَّا **أَنزَلْنَٰهُ** فِى لَيْلَةِ الْقَدْرِ

We have (decided to) reveal this Quran on the night in which fates are decided. (97:1)

Intention

كِتَٰبٌ فُصِّلَتْ ءَايَٰتُهُ قُرْءَانًا عَرَبِيًّا لِّقَوْمٍ يَعْلَمُونَ

This is a Book whose verses have been explained. In the form of an Arabic Quran for <u>those who want to know</u> (41:2)

Expressing the Results

فَخَلَفَ مِنْ بَعْدِهِمْ خَلْفٌ أَضَاعُوا الصَّلَوٰةَ وَ اتَّبَعُوا الشَّهَوَٰتِ فَسَوْفَ يَلْقَوْنَ غَيًّا

Then, after them, those wicked succeeded them who squandered the prayer and followed their desires. So, soon they will face the consequences of going astray. (19:59)

Completeness

يَٰٓأَيُّهَا الَّذِينَ ءَامَنُوٓا **ءَامِنُوا** بِاللّٰهِ وَ رَسُولِهِ وَ الْكِتَٰبِ الَّذِى نَزَّلَ عَلَىٰ رَسُولِهِ

Believers! <u>profess faith</u> in God, in His Messenger and in the Book He has revealed to His Messenger

Examples of the Use of Alif-Laam

The use of Alif-Laam

The use of Alif-Laam on the word *Al-Insaan*

- Here, human beings mean people who have been given the message of Allah (generally all).

وَ وَصَّيْنَا الْإِنْسَانَ بِوَالِدَيْهِ حَمَلَتْهُ أُمُّهُ وَهْنًا عَلَى وَهْنٍ

We have also counseled **human beings** about their parents. His mother kept him in her womb, tolerating distress after distress. (Surah Luqman:14)

- Here, human beings are all humanity in general.

وَ قُلْ لِّعِبَادِيْ يَقُوْلُوا الَّتِيْ هِيَ أَحْسَنُ ۚ إِنَّ الشَّيْطَنَ يَنْزَغُ بَيْنَهُمْ ۚ إِنَّ الشَّيْطَنَ كَانَ لِلْإِنْسَانِ عَدُوًّا مُّبِيْنًا

Tell My servants that [in response to them] they should say what is better. This is because it is Satan who, in the heat of discussion, induces disorder between them. In reality, Satan is an open enemy of **human beings**. (Surah Bani Israel:53)

- Here, a human being means the one who was created.

وَ لَقَدْ خَلَقْنَا الْإِنْسَانَ مِنْ صَلْصَالٍ مِّنْ حَمَإٍ مَّسْنُوْنٍ

We created **human beings** using stinking mud, which sounds. (Surah Al-Hijr:26)

- Allah did not create every human being as described in this verse, but the word Al-Insaan is used. This is used for the first pair (of which Adam and Eve were selected) that represents human beings.

وَ لَقَدْ خَلَقْنَا الْإِنْسَانَ مِنْ سُلَلَةٍ مِّنْ طِيْنٍ

We had created a human being from the essence of clay. (Surah Muminoon:12)

- In the next verse, Allah is speaking about the people of the three nations mentioned in verses 1-3.

لَقَدْ خَلَقْنَا الْإِنْسَانَ فِيْ أَحْسَنِ تَقْوِيْمٍ

Indeed, we created these nations in the best of character (or mold). (Surah Tin:4)

- Here, human beings mean the idolaters whom the Quran addressed directly.

وَ يَقُوْلُ الْاِنْسَانُ ءَ اِذَا مَا مِتُّ لَسَوْفَ اُخْرَجُ حَيًّا

The man says: "Will I be taken out and given life again after I die?" (Surah Maryam:66)

اَللّٰهُ الَّذِىْ خَلَقَ السَّمٰوٰتِ وَ الْاَرْضَ وَ اَنْزَلَ مِنَ السَّمَآءِ مَآءً فَاَخْرَجَ بِهٖ مِنَ الثَّمَرٰتِ رِزْقًا لَّكُمْ ۚ وَ سَخَّرَ لَكُمُ الْفُلْكَ لِتَجْرِىَ فِى الْبَحْرِ بِاَمْرِهٖ ۚ وَ سَخَّرَ لَكُمُ الْاَنْهٰرَ

وَ سَخَّرَ لَكُمُ الشَّمْسَ وَ الْقَمَرَ دَآئِبَيْنِ ۚ وَ سَخَّرَ لَكُمُ الَّيْلَ وَ النَّهَارَ

وَ اٰتٰىكُمْ مِّنْ كُلِّ مَا سَاَلْتُمُوْهُ ۚ وَ اِنْ تَعُدُّوْا نِعْمَتَ اللّٰهِ لَا تُحْصُوْهَا ۚ

اِنَّ الْاِنْسَانَ لَظَلُوْمٌ كَفَّارٌ

God created the heavens and the earth and sent down water from the sky. Then, through it, various fruits were borne for your sustenance, and the ship was put to your service to sail in the sea at His behest. He also put the seas, the sun, and the moon to your service, and they all move continuously. Similarly, day and night are put at your service, giving you everything you ask for. If you would like to count the favors of God, you will not be able to count them. [Even then, you associate partners with Him?] In reality, these human beings are very unjust and very ungrateful. (Surah Ibrahim: 32-34)

- Here, the believers refer only to those who fought for the sake of Allah and helped the Prophet.

يٰۤاَيُّهَا الَّذِيْنَ اٰمَنُوْۤا اَطِيْعُوا اللّٰهَ وَ اَطِيْعُوا الرَّسُوْلَ وَ لَا تُبْطِلُوْۤا اَعْمَالَكُمْ

اِنَّ الَّذِيْنَ كَفَرُوْا وَ صَدُّوْا عَنْ سَبِيْلِ اللّٰهِ ثُمَّ مَاتُوْا وَ هُمْ كُفَّارٌ فَلَنْ يَّغْفِرَ اللّٰهُ لَهُمْ

فَلَا تَهِنُوْا وَ تَدْعُوْۤا اِلَى السَّلْمِ ۖ وَ اَنْتُمُ الْاَعْلَوْنَ ۖ وَ اللّٰهُ مَعَكُمْ وَ لَنْ يَّتِرَكُمْ اَعْمَالَكُمْ

Believers! Obey the directive of God and His Messenger [disregarding everything] and let not your deeds come to nothing [by being unfaithful to God and His Messenger]. There is no doubt that those who denied and stopped [people] from God's path, then died in this state of denial, God shall certainly not forgive them. So, do not show weakness, and those who are now about to be punished do not invite them now to reconciliation, and bear in mind that you alone shall remain dominant. God is with you and shall not show any reduction to you in your deeds. (Surah Muhammad:33-35)

- Here, "believers" refers to a specific group within Muslims.

يَا أَيُّهَا الَّذِينَ اٰمَنُوا لَا تَتَّخِذُوا الْكٰفِرِينَ اَوْلِيَاءَ مِنْ دُونِ الْمُؤْمِنِينَ اَتُرِيدُونَ اَنْ تَجْعَلُوا لِلّٰهِ عَلَيْكُمْ سُلْطٰنًا مُّبِينًا

Believers! [By being misled by them] do not make friends with the disbelievers [of the Prophet] , leaving aside the Muslims. Do you want to give God clear evidence against yourselves? (Surah Nisaa: 144)

- Starting from Verse 135, the qualities required of believers are discussed. At the same time, the behavior of hypocrites is discussed.
- In verse 144, Allah commanded them not to make friends with the disbelievers; otherwise, they would never be able to mend their behavior. Verse 145 also warns them.

اِنَّ الْمُنٰفِقِينَ فِي الدَّرْكِ الْاَسْفَلِ مِنَ النَّارِ

These Hypocrites shall be in the lowest level of Hell
(Surah Nisaa: 145)

- Here, Earth means a specific area or Kingdom on Earth.

قَالَ اجْعَلْنِي عَلٰى خَزَائِنِ الْاَرْضِ ۖ اِنِّي حَفِيظٌ عَلِيمٌ

Joseph said: "Handover the treasures of this land to me because I can protect and also have knowledge." (Surah Yusuf: 55)

- When Prophet Yusuf was released from jail, the King welcomed him and said he would now be his special advisor.
- Upon hearing that Prophet Yusuf requested to be in charge of finance because of the dream that the King saw.
- According to the dream, Egypt was about to face tough years of drought, and Prophet Yusuf believed that, with the help of Allah, he would manage it better than anyone.

The Examples of Oaths

Oaths in the Quran

- Presenting 'A' as a witness/evidence to prove 'B'. Please refer back to the chapter of Oaths in the Quran.

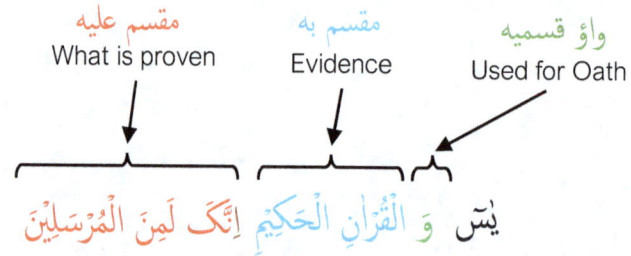

This is Surah Yasin. This Quran, replete with wisdom, bears witness that you surely are among the messengers sent (Surah Ya-Sin:1-3)

- The Quran, full of wisdom, is presented as evidence for proving the Messengerhood of Prophet Muhammad.
- A person who claims to bring this Quran, which anyone can attest to, is full of wisdom and conclusive arguments about Allah, can be no other but a Messenger.

The Examples of the Quran explaining itself

Quran explains itself

Example 1: What is *Al-Hikmah*

- How the Quran explains itself is evident in the meanings of the words Al-Kitaab and Al-Hikmah.
- After reading the usage of these two words in the Quran, a reader can easily understand what they mean when used together.

رَبَّنَا وَ ابْعَثْ فِيهِمْ رَسُوْلًا مِّنْهُمْ يَتْلُوْا عَلَيْهِمْ اٰيٰتِكَ وَ يُعَلِّمُهُمُ الْكِتٰبَ وَ الْحِكْمَةَ وَ يُزَكِّيْهِمْ

Lord! Send forth a messenger from amongst them who reads out to them Your verses, instructs them in the <u>law</u> and <u>wisdom</u>, and as a result, purifies them. (Surah Baqarah: 129)

اِذْ بَعَثَ فِيْهِمْ رَسُوْلًا مِّنْ اَنْفُسِهِمْ يَتْلُوْا عَلَيْهِمْ اٰيٰتِهٖ وَ يُزَكِّيْهِمْ وَ يُعَلِّمُهُمُ الْكِتٰبَ وَ الْحِكْمَةَ

When He sent for them a Messenger from amongst themselves who recites His revelations before them and purifies them, and for this instructs them in the law and the wisdom. (Surah Aal-e-Imran:164)

- Quran has repeated this pair at 2:151, 2:231, 3:48, 3:81, 4:54, 4:113, 5:110, 62:2.
- The word Al-Kitaab is commonly used in Arabic to refer to the Law. So, the Messenger teaches Law. But what is Al-Hikmah exactly? It is often translated as Wisdom. Is it specific wisdom about something or general wisdom?
- The Quran answers that and explains what Al-Hikmah is in Surah Bani Israel.

- God gave us the **Ten Commandments** in the Quran in Surah Bani Israel in Verses 22-39 where the word **Al-Hikmah** is explained.

1. Do not take any deity besides Allah, lest [on the Day of Judgement] you are left blameworthy and disgraceful. And [remember that] your Lord has enjoined you to worship none but Him

2. And treat your parents with kindness. If either or both of them attain old age in your life before you, show them no sign of impatience, nor scold them while answering; but speak to them with good etiquette and treat them with humility and tenderness, and say: "Lord, be merciful to them the way they nursed me in childhood." Your Lord fully knows what is in your hearts; if you remain obedient [to them, then you should know that], He forgives those who turn to Him.

3. And give to the near of kin their due, the destitute, and the traveler. And do not squander your wealth wastefully, for the wasteful are Satan's brothers, and Satan is ever-ungrateful to his Lord. And if you have to disregard [those in need] because you are seeking your Lord's bounty of which you are waiting, then speak to them affectionately. And do not be miserly or prodigal, [that as a result of it] you should either earn reproach or be reduced to indigence. Indeed, your Lord gives abundantly to whom He pleases and sparingly to whom He pleases. He is aware of His servants and is observing them.

4. And do not kill your children for fear of poverty. We provide for them and you because killing them is a heinous crime.

5. And do not even go near adultery because it is blatant lewdness and a very evil path.

6. And do not wrongfully kill any person whose life has been held sacred by God, and remember that if someone is slain unjustly, We have given his heir the authority. He should also not exceed limits in his revenge, given that he has been helped.

7. And do not approach the wealth of orphans except in a just and best manner until they reach maturity.

8. And keep your promises because you shall be held accountable for promises. And give full measure when you measure, and weigh with the correct scales. This is better and fairer as far as the consequences are concerned.

9. And do not go after what you do not know, because eyes, ears, and heart – all of them shall be questioned.

10. And do not walk conceitedly on the earth because neither can you split the earth nor rival the mountains in stature.

Beliefs and Moral are Al-Hikmah

God concluded the Ten Commandments with these statements.

كُلُّ ذَٰلِكَ كَانَ سَيِّئُهُۥ عِندَ رَبِّكَ مَكْرُوهًا ۚ ذَٰلِكَ مِمَّآ أَوْحَىٰٓ إِلَيْكَ رَبُّكَ مِنَ الْحِكْمَةِ

وَلَا تَجْعَلْ مَعَ اللَّهِ إِلَٰهًا آخَرَ فَتُلْقَىٰ فِي جَهَنَّمَ مَلُومًا مَّدْحُورًا

The evil of each of these things to your Lord is very displeasing. These are from the counsels of wisdom which your Lord has revealed to you. Do not take any deity besides Allah, lest [on the Day of Judgement] you will be cast into Hell condemned and rejected.

- After giving the ten commandments of the Quran, God said What I just told you is the *Al-Hikmah*.
- The Ten Commandments consist solely of two aspects: faith in God alone and morals.
- All of Islam's laws (*Al-Kitab*) have wisdom behind them, which is contained in *Al-Hikmah*.
- For example, there is punishment for adultery, but then God instructed as part of *Al-Hikmah* that we should not go near it because it is an evil path that leads to lewdness and the destruction of morals.
- This example highlights an important way to understand the Quran: it's best understood by letting the Quran explain itself. To truly grasp a topic, you need to read through all relevant parts of the Quran, rather than just picking out one section, making assumptions, and concluding something.

Example 2: The true nature of Jinn

The second example is when a reader tries to understand the true nature of Jinn.

وَ إِذْ قُلْنَا لِلْمَلَٰٓئِكَةِ اسْجُدُوا لِآدَمَ فَسَجَدُوٓا إِلَّآ إِبْلِيسَ ۚ أَبَىٰ وَ اسْتَكْبَرَ ۖ وَ كَانَ مِنَ الْكَٰفِرِينَ

And [to understand the trial of human beings in Our scheme] also narrate the incident when We **asked the angels to bow down** to Adam; then **all of them bowed down except Iblis**. He refused, displaying arrogance, and thus became one of the rejecters. (Surah Baqarah:34)

وَ اِذْ قُلْنَا لِلْمَلٰٓئِكَةِ اسْجُدُوْا لِاٰدَمَ فَسَجَدُوْٓا اِلَّآ اِبْلِيْسَؕ اَبٰى وَ اسْتَكْبَرَۘ وَ كَانَ مِنَ الْكٰفِرِيْنَ

And [to understand the trial of human beings in Our scheme] also narrate the incident when We **asked the angels to bow down** to Adam; then **all of them bowed down except Iblis**. He refused, displaying arrogance, and thus became one of the rejecters. (Surah Baqarah:34)

- If we pay close attention to the above two passages of the Quran, a reader can conclude that Jinn are among the Angels.
- However, the matter is different than what is understood from these verses. The Quran explained it.

وَ اِذْ قُلْنَا لِلْمَلٰٓئِكَةِ اسْجُدُوْا لِاٰدَمَ فَسَجَدُوْٓا اِلَّآ اِبْلِيْسَؕ كَانَ مِنَ الْجِنِّ فَفَسَقَ عَنْ اَمْرِ رَبِّهٖؕ

Remember when We directed the angels: "Prostrate before Adam." They prostrated except Iblis. He was <u>among the Jinn</u>. So, he evaded the directive of his Lord. (Surah Kahf:50)

- Upon examining all the verses of the Quran related to this incident, it becomes clear that in the previous verses, the order to prostrate before Adam was actually given to both Angels and Jinns, and it is Iblees, from among the Jinns, who refused.
- The Quran uses the word "Angels" only in those verses because, in Arabic, the term is sometimes used to refer to the dominant group, including other smaller groups.
- The explanation that was missing in the first instance was clarified by the Quran in the second instance.

Example 3: The nature of Night Journey (Israa)

- In the beginning of Surah Israa (or Bani Israel), God said:

سُبْحٰنَ الَّذِىْٓ اَسْرٰى بِعَبْدِهٖ لَيْلًا مِّنَ الْمَسْجِدِ الْحَرَامِ اِلَى الْمَسْجِدِ الْاَقْصَا الَّذِىْ بٰرَكْنَا حَوْلَهٗ لِنُرِيَهٗ مِنْ اٰيٰتِنَاؕ اِنَّهٗ هُوَ السَّمِيْعُ الْبَصِيْرُ

Free of imperfections is the being who <u>one night took His servant</u> from the Sacred Mosque to that Distant Mosque whose surroundings We have blessed so that We can make him observe some of Our signs. Indeed, only He hears and knows all.[(Surah Bani Israel:1)

- The first verse of the Surah does not mention how God "took" the Prophet Muhammad to a far land to show His signs.
- Later in the Surah, God states in verse 60 that the journey described in the first verse was a prophetic vision, not a physical experience.

وَ مَا جَعَلْنَا الرُّءْيَا الَّتِيّ اَرَيْنٰكَ اِلَّا فِتْنَةً لِّلنَّاسِ

And the dream that we have shown you is nothing but a trial for these people ......
(Surah Bani Israel:60)

- It is important to understand that the Prophets' dreams are no ordinary dreams; they are visions.
- God reveals greater realities (in symbolic form) through visions to the Prophets. For example, through the vision of Isra, the Prophet was told that both places of worship (Ka'abah and Bait al Maqdas) will be under Prophet Muhammad's religious leadership.

Collect 1 example of each from the Quran:
  1. Context changes the meaning of the text
  2. Oath in the Quran
  3. The use of Alif-Laam restricted the group
  4. The example of a Metaphor
  5. The sudden shift in the addressee within a verse
  6. God's words inserted in the middle
  7. The Quran explains itself on a topic

Chapter 15

Wisdom and Reasoning Behind Instructions

In this chapter, we will study how the Quran explains the reasoning and wisdom behind its instructions and why they play a critical role in understanding the instructions of the Quran

Introduction

- There are three types of instruction in Islam, and the goal of each is purification.
  - Instructions related to the cleanliness of our bodies
  - Instructions related to our morals
  - Instructions related to food & drinks (what to consume)

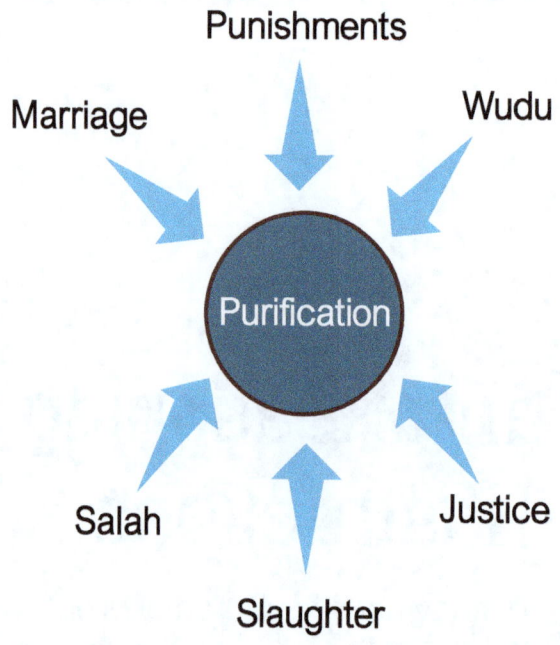

- When a law is described in the Quran (whether it was initiated by the Quran or mentioned because the Prophet had already initiated it), it is often also explained with its wisdom and reasoning. We should pay attention to that when reading the Quran because it helps us understand the instructions and their goals.
- This is especially true when the law is given permanently to Muslims to follow until the Day of Judgment, rather than as a temporary law.
- Several verses in the Quran also encourage contemplation and critical thinking about the natural world and divine laws, suggesting that understanding the rationale is a part of faith and leads to a stronger faith and a deeper connection with God.
- A few such examples from the Quran are discussed in this chapter to help us approach the Quran more effectively and benefit from it.

1. Fasting

يَٰٓأَيُّهَا ٱلَّذِينَ ءَامَنُوا۟ كُتِبَ عَلَيْكُمُ ٱلصِّيَامُ كَمَا كُتِبَ عَلَى ٱلَّذِينَ مِن قَبْلِكُمْ لَعَلَّكُمْ تَتَّقُونَ

Believers! The fast has been made obligatory upon you as it was made obligatory upon those before you, so that you become God-conscious. (Surah Baqarah:183)

- The main reason for prescribing fasting is to increase our consciousness of God.
- All worship rituals are designed to purify the heart and mind.
- To attain purity of heart and mind, one must be God-conscious, which is precisely what fasting does for us.
- God's consciousness allows people to take control of their desires.
- Fasting is the ultimate manifestation of obedience in front of God, resulting from an increased consciousness of Him.
- We don't need to look outside of the Quran to ask this question: Why do we fast? The Quran provides the wisdom behind the prescription for fasting.
- Even if there are no physical benefits of fasting, we will still fast.

2. Qisaas for Murder

وَ لَكُمْ فِى ٱلْقِصَاصِ حَيَوٰةٌ يَٰٓأُو۟لِى ٱلْأَلْبَابِ لَعَلَّكُمْ تَتَّقُونَ

There is LIFE for you in Qisaas, O people of insight, so that you may keep following the limits set by God. (Surah Baqarah:179)

- The word Qisaas in Islamic Law is the punishment prescribed for someone who has intentionally or unintentionally injured or killed another human being.
- The extreme form is the death penalty if the relatives of the deceased refuse to forgive the killer.
- Allah told Muslim rulers enforcing this punishment that there is Life for the community or society in this punishment.
- If they stop punishing killers, it will encourage people to commit murders, which will be a disaster for society.
- In the 21st century, people are against the death penalty, and modern societies are paying the price for this behavior.

3. Financial contract witnesses

يَا أَيُّهَا الَّذِينَ اٰمَنُوا إِذَا تَدَايَنْتُمْ بِدَيْنٍ إِلٰى أَجَلٍ مُّسَمًّى فَاكْتُبُوهُ -----

---- وَ اسْتَشْهِدُوا شَهِيدَيْنِ مِنْ رِّجَالِكُمْ ۚ فَإِنْ لَّمْ يَكُونَا رَجُلَيْنِ فَرَجُلٌ وَّ امْرَاَتٰنِ مِمَّنْ تَرْضَوْنَ مِنَ الشُّهَدَآءِ اَنْ تَضِلَّ اِحْدٰىهُمَا فَتُذَكِّرَ اِحْدٰىهُمَا الْاُخْرٰى ۚ وَ لَا يَأْبَ الشُّهَدَآءُ اِذَا مَا دُعُوا

Believers! When you acquire a loan for a fixed period, record it in writing…….. And call in two male witnesses from among your men, but if two men cannot be found, then one man and two women from among your likable witnesses. Two women, because if one gets confused, the other reminds her. And these witnesses must not refuse when they are summoned. (Surah Baqarah: 282)

- Allah has asked Muslims to keep a record of their loan transactions. Financial matters often raise conflicts if not addressed in writing.
- This advice from Allah is not intended as instructions for us to protect our money and avoid conflicts later.
- Allah has instructed believers to have two male witnesses present when drafting a loan contract.
- Financial matters are complex, and when a conflict arises, witnesses will be asked to come forward and present themselves in court.
- Allah has asked believers to take one male and two females as witnesses if they cannot find two males for any reason.
- Allah gave the reason for selecting two females, "two women because if one gets confused (or forgets), the other reminds her."
- In those days, women were primarily homemakers and rarely involved in external affairs, including financial matters.
- In today's society, we can have a well-educated female witness who can handle financial matters and appear in court without issues when a conflict arises.

Some interpreters of the Quran and Islamic scholars have extended this instruction or advice to other matters. They claim that the Quran has given us a principle that the testimony of two females is equal to that of one male. This is not the right conclusion, as the context of the verses shows. Firstly, it is only about financial matters. Secondly, it is advice. Thirdly, if the reason of "one getting confused so the other can remind" does not apply to a witness, then one female witness is enough.

4. Inheritance

يُوصِيكُمُ اللهُ فِىٓ أَوْلَادِكُمْ ۖ لِلذَّكَرِ مِثْلُ حَظِّ الْأُنثَيَيْنِ ۚ فَإِن كُنَّ نِسَآءً فَوْقَ اثْنَتَيْنِ فَلَهُنَّ ثُلُثَا مَا تَرَكَ ۖ وَ إِن كَانَتْ وَاحِدَةً فَلَهَا النِّصْفُ ۚ وَ لِأَبَوَيْهِ لِكُلِّ وَاحِدٍ مِّنْهُمَا السُّدُسُ مِمَّا تَرَكَ إِن كَانَ لَهُ وَلَدٌ ۚ فَإِن لَّمْ يَكُن لَّهُ وَلَدٌ وَ وَرِثَهُ أَبَوَاهُ فَلِأُمِّهِ الثُّلُثُ ۚ فَإِن كَانَ لَهُ إِخْوَةٌ فَلِأُمِّهِ السُّدُسُ ۚ مِنۢ بَعْدِ وَصِيَّةٍ يُّوصِى بِهَآ أَوْ دَيْنٍ ۗ ءَابَآؤُكُمْ وَ أَبْنَآؤُكُمْ لَا تَدْرُونَ أَيُّهُمْ أَقْرَبُ لَكُمْ نَفْعًا ۚ فَرِيضَةً مِّنَ اللهِ ۗ إِنَّ اللهَ كَانَ عَلِيمًا حَكِيمًا

God directs you regarding (inheritance of) your children, saying that a boy's share equals that of two girls. Then, if there are only girls among the children and there are two or more than two, they shall be given two-thirds of the inheritance, and if there is only one girl, then her share is one-half. But a sixth of the inheritance [before this] should be given to each of the parents of the deceased if he has children; and if there are no children and only parents are the heirs, then his mother's share is a third, and the rest is for his father. However, if he has brothers and sisters, the mother's share is the same one-sixth, and the father's share is the same. These shares should be given after the execution of any will he may have bequeathed and after discharging any [outstanding] debts. [I am distributing this inheritance because] you do not know who among your parents and children is the nearest to you in benefit. For precisely this reason, these shares have been fixed by God, who is Wise and All-Knowing. (Surah Nisaa: 11)

- In Islam, there is a law governing the distribution of inheritance among the deceased's direct relatives.
- Unless someone has made a Will to be executed after his/her death, all distribution happens as per the ratio already defined by Allah in the Quran.
- In other cultures and historically, people used to leave the inheritance to the older male child. That is not a fair way to distribute an inheritance.
- As human beings, we have our personal inclinations and preferences that sometimes get in the way of being just among our blood relatives.
- For this reason, Allah, our Creator, allocated the portions Himself in the Quran.
- However, he did not allocate the portions, providing no rationale.
- He told us in these verses that He has allocated these ratios based on the financial (or other) benefits we receive from each other.
- For example, what benefits does a child receive from his father, or what does a father receive from his male child vs. a female child?
- However, He has also allowed us to write a Will if we see that these benefits are not as they should be.

5. Purpose of prayers

اِنَّنِیۤ اَنَا اللّٰهُ لَاۤ اِلٰهَ اِلَّاۤ اَنَا فَاعْبُدْنِیۙ ۖ وَ اَقِمِ الصَّلٰوةَ لِذِكْرِیۤ

Undoubtedly, I am God; there is no deity besides Me. So, worship Me and be diligent in your prayers to remember Me (in your daily life). (Surah Taha:14)

- The status monotheism occupies in beliefs is the same as the prayer occupies in deeds.
- The prayer is the foremost consequence of the understanding of God.
- This understanding should evoke in a person feelings of love and gratitude towards the Almighty.
- It is not possible for a person to forget Allah after this.
- For example, we love our parents, spend time with them, and call or help them out of gratitude for all they've done for us.
- This is exactly how our relationship with Allah is; prayers are that medium of remembrance.

6. Etiquette of modesty in front of the opposite gender

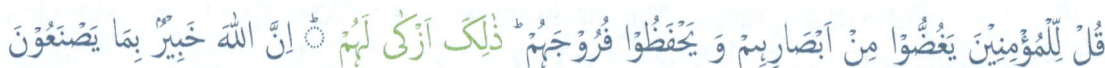

قُلْ لِّلْمُؤْمِنِیْنَ یَغُضُّوْا مِنْ اَبْصَارِهِمْ وَ یَحْفَظُوْا فُرُوْجَهُمْ ؕ ذٰلِكَ اَزْكٰی لَهُمْ ؕ اِنَّ اللّٰهَ خَبِیْرٌۢ بِمَا یَصْنَعُوْنَ

[O Prophet!] Tell these believers to restrain their eyes and guard their private parts [if women are present in these houses]. This is a purer way for them. Undoubtedly, God is well aware of whatever they do. (Surah Nur:30)

- Allah has asked Muslim men and women in the Quran to restrain their eyes and guard their chastity.
- He started the instructions with men, but the exact instructions were also given to women.
- Before talking to Muslim women, Allah describes why He is instructing them to restrain their eyes and guard their chastity – to gain purity of their hearts.
- These etiquettes nurture the purity of hearts and create a healthy society where chastity, respect, and righteousness are at the center.
- As long as these etiquettes are observed, we can engage in our social activities, because Allah does not want us to be socially isolated.

Assignment

Find a few verses in the Quran where Allah mentioned the reason why He gave that instruction or advice.

Chapter 16

The Quran's approach to human beings

In this chapter, we will examine how the Quran approaches human beings and the guidance it offers them.

The Quran's Approach

- The Quran does not approach humans in isolation but relates its guidance to the following:
    - a priori knowledge they already possess
    - common sense
    - history
    - intellect

Inner (pre-revelation) guidance

Human beings are endowed with knowledge, five senses, and common sense from birth. For example, you can easily distinguish round shapes from square ones from a very early age. If there is a sign for a bus stop, then you would know without experimenting with anything that the next bus would stop here.

Previous Scriptures

The Quran is the last book of God, not the first one. It refers to previous books known in history. So, when the Quran discusses incidents related to Prophet Musa, it leaves the details to be inferred, assuming people would consult the Torah or the Bible for further information.

Reason not dogma

It appeals to the human intellect and the ability to reason instead of giving a dogma to believe in. For example, even for the most fundamental beliefs like monotheism, the Quran uses reason and logic to argue in favor of monotheism instead of forcing people to believe in one God.

The Quran consistently calls on its readers to employ reason and reflection, drawing upon both universal truths (*a priori* knowledge) and lessons from common sense and history, making it impossible to fully comprehend without these intellectual tools.

Dogma: A set of core assumptions or beliefs that are considered established and accepted without question.

1. Pre-Revelatory Guidance

- The Quran emphasizes the fact that humans were not created blind and dumb. They have a faculty called intuition or common sense, and the ability to distinguish between good and evil. This is fundamental to receiving and comprehending the revelation.

وَ نَفْسٍ وَّ مَا سَوّٰهَا ۙ فَاَلْهَمَهَا فُجُوْرَهَا وَ تَقْوٰىهَا ۙ قَدْ اَفْلَحَ مَنْ زَكّٰىهَا ۙ وَ قَدْ خَابَ مَنْ دَسّٰىهَا

And the soul and the way it is perfected, then inspired it with its evil and its good that the Day of Judgement is certain to come; hence, he succeeded who purified his soul, and he failed who corrupted it. (Shams: 7-10)

وَ هَدَيْنٰهُ النَّجْدَيْنِ

And have We not **shown him** the two paths (so he could tell between good and evil) (Balad: 3)

اِنَّا هَدَيْنٰهُ السَّبِيْلَ اِمَّا شَاكِرًا وَّ اِمَّا كَفُوْرًا

We **showed him the (good and evil) path**. It is now up to him to be grateful or profess disbelief. (Insaan: 3)

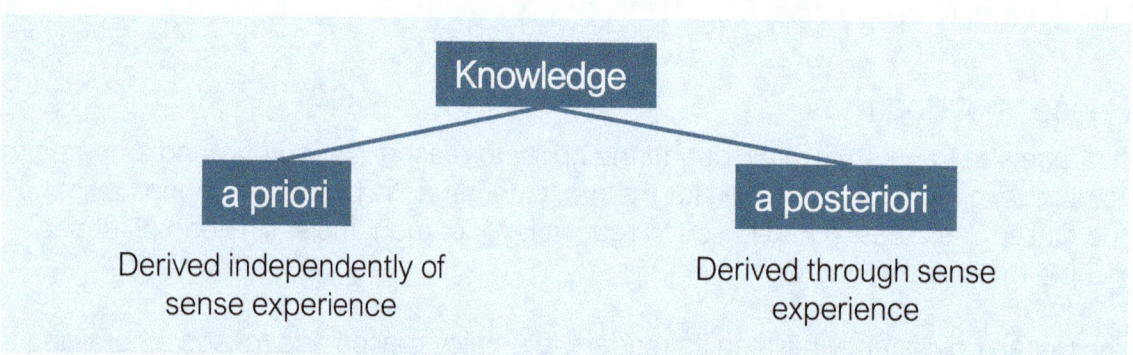

- The same word, *Ilham,* which is used for pre-revelatory guidance, is also used for Wahi, and it is shared among humanity.
- When it comes to common sense and intuition, we all speak the same language.
- Human beings are asked to use their intuition, common sense, and knowledge even when approaching the text revealed by God.
- A priori includes many things: the sense of size (small vs. big), distance, part or complete, common math, logical reasoning, deduction, etc. Similarly, the concept of good and evil is also part of it.
- God showed us both paths and gave us free will to make moral choices.

Relationship with Revelation

Pre-Revelatory Guidance	Revelatory Guidance
Sets the foundation for recognizing the Creator, His prophets, revelations, concepts of good and evil, right and wrong	Details on how to build a relationship with that Creator, how to worship Him, details about religion, guidance on things where we might err, and how to lead a righteous life

- The revelatory guidance continually reminds the person to heed the pre-revelatory guidance they received.
- It is like being in a dark room: you must first use a torch (intuition) to find the light switch before you fully brighten the room (revelation).

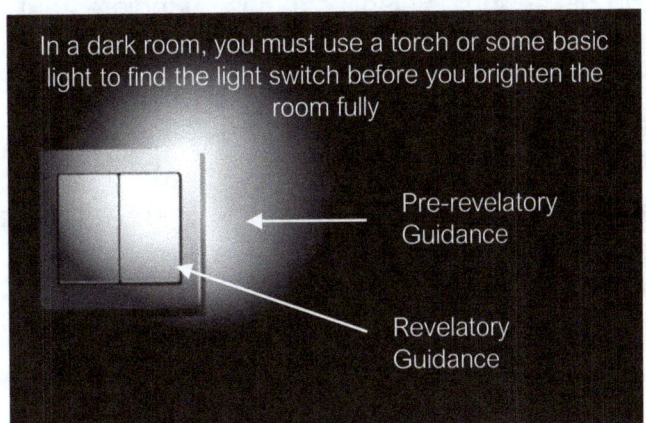

In a dark room, you must use a torch or some basic light to find the light switch before you brighten the room fully

Pre-revelatory Guidance

Revelatory Guidance

- Surah Noor, Ayah 35, highlights this relationship through a beautiful parable.

اَللّٰهُ نُوْرُ السَّمٰوٰتِ وَ الْاَرْضِ ۖ مَثَلُ نُوْرِهٖ كَمِشْكٰوةٍ فِيْهَا مِصْبَاحٌ ۖ اَلْمِصْبَاحُ فِيْ زُجَاجَةٍ ۖ اَلزُّجَاجَةُ كَاَنَّهَا كَوْكَبٌ دُرِّيٌّ يُّوْقَدُ مِنْ شَجَرَةٍ مُّبٰرَكَةٍ زَيْتُوْنَةٍ لَّا شَرْقِيَّةٍ وَّ لَا غَرْبِيَّةٍ ۙ يَّكَادُ زَيْتُهَا يُضِيْٓءُ وَ لَوْ لَمْ تَمْسَسْهُ نَارٌ ۗ نُوْرٌ عَلٰى نُوْرٍ ۗ يَهْدِى اللّٰهُ لِنُوْرِهٖ مَنْ يَّشَآءُ ۚ وَ يَضْرِبُ اللّٰهُ الْاَمْثَالَ لِلنَّاسِ ۗ وَ اللّٰهُ بِكُلِّ شَيْءٍ عَلِيْمٌ

[The parable is that] God is the light of the heavens and the earth. [In the heart of a person,] the example of this light of His is as if a niche has a lamp. The lamp is in crystal. The crystal is like a shining star. It is lit up by oil from a lush olive tree, which is neither eastern nor western. Its oil is [so transparent] as if it will light up even without fire touching it. Light upon light. God grants this light of His guidance to whomsoever He wills. God mentions these parables to guide people and is aware of everything. (Surah Noor:35)

Relationship with Revelation

Faith in God provides light and direction

- **Faith in God:** The core message of Surah Noor Verse 35 is that faith in God provides light and clarity in life, while a lack of faith leaves a person in darkness, uncertain of their purpose. Life without faith is like walking in the dark.

- **Without belief in God, the world can feel meaningless:** You can't truly understand why the universe was created or what your personal purpose is.

- **It's like being lost:** When you're unsure about life's big questions—like what is truly good or bad, and whether your actions matter—you wander without a clear destination. The questions do not go away, but then, in the absence of God, you try to find the answers and get vague and incorrect answers to satisfy the desire of having answers for those questions.

- **It helps answer the big questions:** With faith, questions about your purpose, accountability, and the difference between right and wrong become clear.

- **Belief in God and His attributes clarifies things:** As pointed out earlier, it's like turning on a light in a dark room. You can suddenly gain a deeper understanding of the universe and your place within it.

- **It guides your every step:** For a believer, faith-guidance illuminates your path, so you move forward with confidence and purpose.

- **Ultimately, true guidance comes from God:** The Quran has a powerful message: "He whom God does not give light, for him there is no light". It's a reminder that true, lasting guidance can only come from Allah.

2. Previous Scriptures

- The second thing the Quran relates its guidance to is the background of all the religious scriptures, which nations like Jews and Christians are well aware of.

- The Quran insists that the Quran is the last book of God, not the first, and Prophet Muhammad is the last Prophet of God, not the first.

- The picture on the next page shows the history of religious scriptures and their timeline.

The Quran discusses these previous scriptures, and their central guidance is the same as the Quran's, although the details differ.

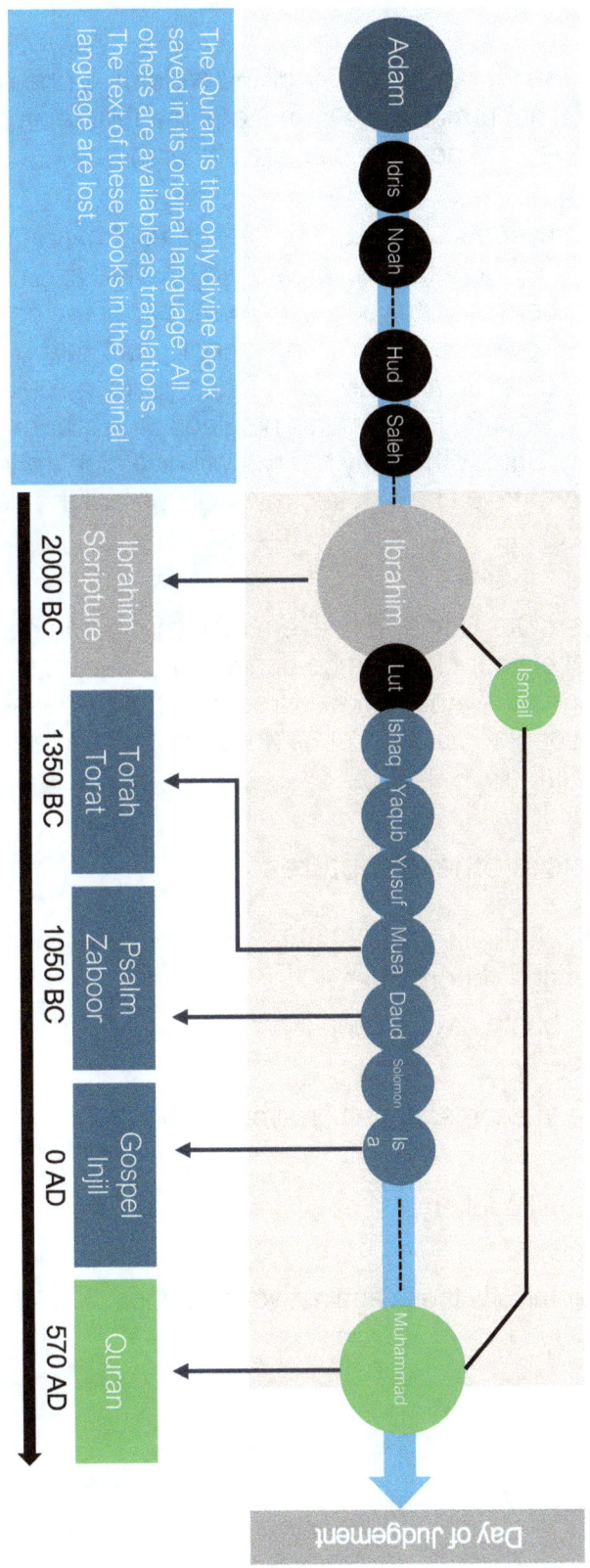

The Quran is the only divine book saved in its original language. All others are available as translations. The text of these books in the original language are lost.

	Adam
	Idris
	Noah
	Hud
	Saleh
	Ibrahim
	Ismail
	Lut
	Ishaq
	Yaqub
	Yusuf
	Musa
	Daud
	Solomon
	Isa
	Muhammad

2000 BC	Ibrahim Scripture
1350 BC	Torah Torat
1050 BC	Psalm Zaboor
0 AD	Gospel Injil
570 AD	Quran

Day of Judgement

Guidance in other scriptures

Surah Fatihah

- The main theme of the Quran and other divine scriptures (the part attributed to the Prophet of that time) remains the same, and matters related to morality and faith have not changed. Some examples are shown here:

O Lord, listen to my prayer and take note of the sound of my requests. On the day of my trouble, I send up my cry to you, for you will give me an answer. There is no god like you, O Lord; there are no works like yours. Let all the nations you have made come and worship you, O Lord, giving glory to your name. You are great and do great works of wonder; you are only God. Make your way clear to me, O Lord; I will go on my way in your faith: let my heart be glad in the fear of your name. I will praise you, O Lord my God, with all my heart; I will give glory to your name forever. Your mercy to me is great; you have taken my soul up from the deep places of the underworld. (Psalm 86)

Let this be your prayer: Our Father in heaven, may your name be kept holy. Let your kingdom come. Let your pleasure be done, as in heaven, so on earth. Give us this day bread for our needs. And make us free of our debts, as we have made those free who are in debt to us. And let us not be put to the test, but keep us safe from the Evil One. (Matthew, 6:9-13)

Ten Commandments in other scriptures

1. You shall have no other gods before me.
2. Honor your father and your mother.
3. Remember the Sabbath day, to keep it holy.
4. You shall not make idols.
5. You shall not take the name of the Lord your God in vain.
6. You shall not kill.
7. You shall not commit adultery.
8. You shall not steal.
9. You shall not bear false witness against your neighbor.
10. You shall not covet.

Importance of Charity in other scriptures

Make no store of wealth for yourselves on earth, where it may be turned to dust by worms and weather, and thieves may come in by force and take it away. But make a store for yourselves in heaven, where it will not be turned to dust and thieves do not come in to take it away: For where your wealth is, there will your heart be. (Matthew 6:19-21)

Quran validates previous scriptures

اِنَّاۤ اَنْزَلْنَا التَّوْرٰىةَ فِيْهَا هُدًى وَّ نُوْرٌ

وَ كَيْفَ يُحَكِّمُوْنَكَ وَ عِنْدَهُمُ التَّوْرٰىةُ فِيْهَا حُكْمُ اللّٰهِ

We have revealed this Torah, in which there was both guidance and light. (Maida:44)

How do they make you give a verdict even though they have the Torah with them, which contains God's verdict? (Maida:43)

وَ قَفَّيْنَا عَلٰۤى اٰثَارِهِمْ بِعِيْسَى ابْنِ مَرْيَمَ مُصَدِّقًا لِّمَا بَيْنَ يَدَيْهِ مِنَ التَّوْرٰىةِ وَ اٰتَيْنٰهُ الْاِنْجِيْلَ فِيْهِ هُدًى وَّ نُوْرٌ ۙ وَّ مُصَدِّقًا لِّمَا بَيْنَ يَدَيْهِ مِنَ التَّوْرٰىةِ وَ هُدًى وَّ مَوْعِظَةً لِّلْمُتَّقِيْنَ

In the footsteps of these [messengers], We sent forth Jesus, son of Mary, who corroborated the already present Torah. And We gave him the Gospel in which there was guidance and light. It also corroborated the Torah present before it as a guide and an admonition for the God-fearing and with the directive (Maida:46)

اَلَّذِيْنَ يَتَّبِعُوْنَ الرَّسُوْلَ النَّبِيَّ الْاُمِّيَّ الَّذِيْ يَجِدُوْنَهٗ مَكْتُوْبًا عِنْدَهُمْ فِى التَّوْرٰىةِ وَ الْاِنْجِيْلِ

[for those] who [today] will follow this messenger, this unlettered prophet whose mention they see written in the Torah and the Gospel. He directs them to do good and forbids them from evil (Aaraf:157)

- This is the reason the Quran omits many historical details in the stories of the prophets, assuming that its addressees are familiar with them from their own scriptures.
- Scholars of Islam have used earlier divine scriptures as a supplementary source of information or for details of specific incidents that the Quran is not explicit about.

3. Quran promotes reason and thinking

- The Quran places a significant emphasis on appealing to human intellect and reason. It underscores the importance of reflection, understanding, and reason in the pursuit of knowledge and truth, as described in the Quran.

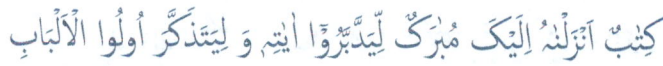

وَ مَا يَذَّكَّرُ اِلَّآ اُولُوا الْاَلْبَابِ

كِتٰبٌ اَنْزَلْنٰهُ اِلَيْكَ مُبٰرَكٌ لِّيَدَّبَّرُوْٓا اٰيٰتِهٖ وَ لِيَتَذَكَّرَ اُولُوا الْاَلْبَابِ

Yet none but men of wisdom receive a reminder [from such things] (2:269)

It is a blessed book that We have revealed to you [O Prophet] so that people ponder its verses and those endowed with intellect are reminded of it.(38:29)

اِنَّ فِيْ خَلْقِ السَّمٰوٰتِ وَ الْاَرْضِ وَ اخْتِلَافِ الَّيْلِ وَ النَّهَارِ لَاٰيٰتٍ لِّاُولِى الْاَلْبَابِ

In reality, in the creation of the heavens and the earth and in the alternation of night and day, there are many signs for people of insight (3:190)

Encouragement of Reflection and Contemplation:

The Quran frequently encourages individuals to reflect on the natural world, human experience, and the signs of God in the universe. Verses often begin with phrases like "Do they not see?" "Have they not considered?" and "Do they not think?" urge readers to use their intellect to understand the divine message.

Questioning and Debate:

The Quran includes numerous questions posed to provoke thought and discussion. These questions challenge assumptions, clarify concepts, and lead to deeper understanding, such as "Were they created by nothing, or were they the creators [of themselves]?"

Use of Parables and Analogies:

The Quran employs parables and analogies to make complex ideas more accessible and to illustrate moral and religious lessons.

Rational Arguments:

The Quran presents logical arguments to support its theological and ethical teachings. It addresses common doubts and objections, providing reasoned responses that appeal to the intellect. For example, "Had there been gods within the heavens and earth besides Allah, they both would have been ruined."

Promotes self-reflection

- The Quran promotes self-reflection by encouraging readers to examine their own attitudes and reactions in different circumstances.

لَا يَسْـَٔمُ الْإِنْسَانُ مِنْ دُعَاءِ الْخَيْرِ ۖ وَ اِنْ مَّسَّهُ الشَّرُّ فَيَـُٔوْسٌ قَنُوْطٌ
وَ لَئِنْ اَذَقْنَاهُ رَحْمَةً مِّنَّا مِنْۢ بَعْدِ ضَرَّآءَ مَسَّتْهُ لَيَقُوْلَنَّ هٰذَا لِیْ ۙ وَ مَآ اَظُنُّ السَّاعَةَ قَآئِمَةً ۙ وَّ لَئِنْ رُّجِعْتُ
اِلٰی رَبِّیْۤ اِنَّ لِیْ عِنْدَهٗ لَلْحُسْنٰی ۚ فَلَنُنَبِّئَنَّ الَّذِیْنَ كَفَرُوْا بِمَا عَمِلُوْا ۗ وَ لَنُذِیْقَنَّهُمْ مِّنْ عَذَابٍ غَلِیْظٍ

[Strange is the matter of] human beings; [when hardships come his way,] he does not get tired of supplicating for goodness; but if he is faced with a calamity [and sees that his supplications are not being answered,] he loses hope and despairs. And, if after that calamity which has afflicted him, We make him taste Our mercy, he will definitely say: "This is what I deserve, and I do not think that the Hereafter will happen but [if it is assumed to happen and] I am returned to my Lord, there is no doubt that there too good awaits me." [These are their dreams on the basis of which they are making fun of the Prophet.] So, We shall definitely inform these disbelievers of their deeds and shall definitely make them taste a stern torment. (Surah HaaMeem Sajdah 41: 49-50)

- The Quran describes various human reactions—fear, arrogance, despair, and gratitude—that help readers recognize their own tendencies.
- Contrast Between Times of Ease and Hardship – The Quran shows how people may forget Allah in times of ease and turn to Him in times of hardship, prompting reflection on spiritual consistency.

Example: "And when adversity touches man, he calls upon Us; then when We bestow on him a favor from Us, he says, 'I have only been given it because of [my] knowledge.'" (Surah Az-Zumar 39:49)

- Our Iman in Allah SWT cannot be controlled by the situations of ease and difficulties – we must remember, ease and difficulty both come from Him, and part of our test in this life.

Quran relies on human intellect

- God provides universal principles, moral boundaries, and broad directives, and then the discussion of detailed systems, such as the political or economic system, is left to human intellect, ijtihad, and collective wisdom.

وَ الَّذِينَ اسْتَجَابُوا لِرَبِّهِمْ وَ أَقَامُوا الصَّلوةَ ۚ وَ أَمْرُهُمْ شُوْرٰى بَيْنَهُمْ ۚ وَ مِمَّا رَزَقْنٰهُمْ يُنْفِقُوْنَ

And those who have responded to the invitation of their Lord and are diligent in the prayer, and their system is based on their mutual consultation, and they spend [for Our cause] from the sustenance We have blessed them with. (42:31)

يٰٓأَيُّهَا الَّذِينَ اٰمَنُوْا كُوْنُوْا قَوّٰمِيْنَ بِالْقِسْطِ شُهَدَآءَ لِلّٰهِ وَ لَوْ عَلٰٓى اَنْفُسِكُمْ اَوِ الْوَالِدَيْنِ وَ الْاَقْرَبِيْنَ

Believers! Adhere to justice, bearing witness to it for God, even if this evidence is against yourselves, your parents, and your kinsfolk. 4:135)

وَ لَا تَأْكُلُوْا اَمْوَالَكُمْ بَيْنَكُمْ بِالْبَاطِلِ

And do not consume each other's wealth in unjust and wrong ways (2:111)

يٰٓأَيُّهَا الَّذِينَ اٰمَنُوْا لَا تَأْكُلُوا الرِّبٰوٓا اَضْعَافًا مُضٰعَفَةً ۖ وَ اتَّقُوا اللّٰهَ لَعَلَّكُمْ تُفْلِحُوْنَ

Believers! do not consume this interest, doubling it many times over, and keep fearing God that you may prosper. (3:130)

- The Quran does not prescribe a full political system (like democracy, monarchy, etc.). It gives the principle of mutual consultation, leaving societies free to choose forms of governance as long as the consultation and justice are upheld.
- The Quran sets justice as a non-negotiable principle for a society to prosper, but does not dictate every detail of judicial procedures. Those are developed by human societies and jurists.
- Similarly, the Quran does not provide any banking or financial system. It simply lays down the ethical foundation and limits: do not unjustly consume people's wealth or do so through crooked means, and stay away from Riba (usury). Trade is fine, but no business should be set up to burden others with usury; it should leave it to humans to design financial instruments consistent with these principles.

Assignment

1. Find a few verses in the Quran where Allah mentions various human attitudes and reactions in this life for them to ponder and self-reflect.

2. Read the verses of Surah Hashr 6-8 and ponder how these verses set the foundation for a welfare state that takes care of the unprivileged in a society.

Chapter 17

Al-Insaan in the Quran

In this chapter, we will study the use of the word Al-Insaan in the Quran, as many interpreters translate it as "human beings".

The use of الإنْسَان in the Quran

- A common view among Quran translators is that when the Quran uses the word Al-Insaan, it refers to human beings in general. However, this is not the case, as we will see through the examples in the Quran. The Quran uses the word Al-Insaan for three types of people:

- The three types of people that the Quran uses the word Al-Insaan for are described in the picture above:
  - Certain people lived during the time when the Quran was being revealed.
  - Certain groups or societies from the past are used as examples in the Quran.
  - And also the universal characteristics shared by all of humanity.
- Within these groups, the Quran discussed their origins, their attitude towards the messengers of God, and their fate and destiny due to their behavior.
- This is quite a common use of the words "man" and "human being" in English.
  - The **men** put up a great fight on the pitch today. It refers strictly to the members of that specific sports team, not all males on Earth.
  - Don't let the **man** keep you down. Here, "the man" specifically means the government, corporate bosses, or the establishment.
  - While criticizing someone without calling them out, we say, "What's wrong with **humans/people** these days?"
  - The imam on the pulpit, when talking to the congregation, says "O **people** ...." He does not mean all the people on earth.

Note: In all the verses, masculine nouns and pronouns are used, but they refer to human beings in general, including both men and women.

Examples of the usage

Group among direct addressees – Example 1

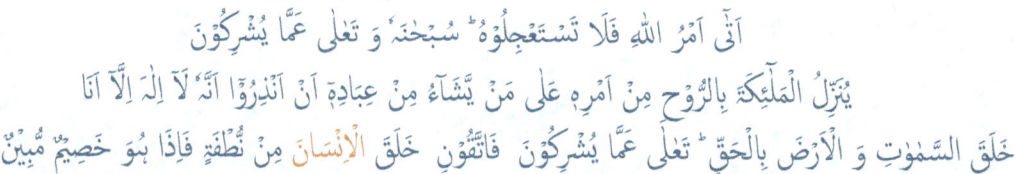

اَتّى اَمْرُ اللهِ فَلَا تَسْتَعْجِلُوْهُ ۚ سُبْحٰنَهٗ وَ تَعٰلٰى عَمَّا يُشْرِكُوْنَ

يُنَزِّلُ الْمَلٰٓئِكَةَ بِالرُّوْحِ مِنْ اَمْرِهٖ عَلٰى مَنْ يَّشَآءُ مِنْ عِبَادِهٖ اَنْ اَنْذِرُوْۤا اَنَّهٗ لَآ اِلٰهَ اِلَّاۤ اَنَا

خَلَقَ السَّمٰوٰتِ وَ الْاَرْضَ بِالْحَقِّ ۚ تَعٰلٰى عَمَّا يُشْرِكُوْنَ فَاتَّقُوْنِ خَلَقَ الْاِنْسَانَ مِنْ نُّطْفَةٍ فَاِذَا هُوَ خَصِيْمٌ مُّبِيْنٌ

The command of God has been pronounced. So, do not seek to hasten it. He is pure and exalted from the things they associate with Him. [Tell them, O Prophet, that not everyone is worthy that God send down angels to him.] He sends down angels with the command of revelation to whomsoever He wills with the directive: "Warn people: 'There is no deity [for you] except Me; so, fear Me alone.'" He has created the heavens and the earth with truth. [No one can influence His decisions.] He is far above those things which they associate with Him. He has created man with a small drop (of fluid), but you see that he (the opposition) has stood to become an open enemy (to Me). (Surah Nahl: 1-4)

- Right after these verses, God spoke of the blessings He had given to His addressees.
- In mentioning these blessings, cattle are mentioned first because they were the primary source of wealth for the Arabs.
- They derived most of their clothing, food, and other benefits from them, and cattle were also a matter of prestige at that time.
- In those days, someone with many cattle was considered rich, blessed, and honored in society.
- Ideally, in return, they must recognize that the Bestower is exceedingly Kind and Gracious.
- The necessary conclusion is to acknowledge the Creator's rights, become a grateful servant, remain active in His obedience, not associate others in His rights, and not stand as a rival against Him.
- Yet God said that a strange misfortune occurs: upon receiving God's blessings, instead of becoming grateful, these people are consumed by their own ego and challenge God's messenger, which is equivalent to challenging God.
- Here, the word Al-Insaan refers to those who forgot their birth and how meaningless they were before it, but now they are up against the Creator. They are the direct addressees of the Prophet and the message as it was revealed.

Example 2

اِنَّ هٰذَا الْقُرْاٰنَ يَهْدِىْ لِلَّتِىْ هِىَ اَقْوَمُ وَ يُبَشِّرُ الْمُؤْمِنِيْنَ الَّذِيْنَ يَعْمَلُوْنَ الصّٰلِحٰتِ اَنَّ لَهُمْ اَجْرًا كَبِيْرًا

وَّ اَنَّ الَّذِيْنَ لَا يُؤْمِنُوْنَ بِالْاٰخِرَةِ اَعْتَدْنَا لَهُمْ عَذَابًا اَلِيْمًا ۞ وَ يَدْعُ الْاِنْسَانُ بِالشَّرِّ دُعَاۤءَهٗ بِالْخَيْرِ ۗ وَ كَانَ الْاِنْسَانُ عَجُوْلًا

[People!] In reality, this Quran shows the way that is absolutely straight. It gives glad tidings to the believers who do righteous deeds, for them is a great reward, and this also that those who do not believe in the Hereafter, for them We have prepared a painful torment. [They ask for its sign.] Man [regrettably] asks for good [for himself,] in the same way as he asks for evil (without knowing the consequences). Man is very impatient. (Surah Israa: 9-11)

- God told the disbelievers and the People of the Book that they should adopt the path that the Quran calls toward instead of wandering through twisted and winding valleys.
- It gives glad tidings of a Great Reward to those who believe and adopt a life of righteous deeds.
- As for those who do not believe in the Hereafter and reject the Quran because of that, there is a painful punishment prepared for them.
- After that, God describes the state of the Quran's opponents who, instead of believing, were demanding a 'sign of punishment.' This was because the Messenger was threatening them with punishment in this world before their eyes.
- Since this demand was utterly foolish and deadly for them, the address turns away from them to state generally and regretfully: 'Man's condition is strange; he prays for evil and destruction with the same fervor he should use to seek good.' Instead of using the respite they've been granted to improve their lives, they wish to see the very punishment they are being warned about as quickly as possible.
- The disbelievers of Prophet Muhammad were making such a foolish demand out of arrogance.
- Although the Quran speaks about the specific group the Prophet was addressing, we can see similar behavior in our lives. Arrogant people, when warned of consequences for their bad behavior, ask to have the consequences brought upon them instead of mending their ways.

Example 3

اِقْرَأْ بِاسْمِ رَبِّكَ الَّذِىْ خَلَقَ ۚ ﴿١﴾ خَلَقَ الْاِنْسَانَ مِنْ عَلَقٍ ۚ ﴿٢﴾ اِقْرَأْ وَ رَبُّكَ الْاَكْرَمُ ۙ ﴿٣﴾ الَّذِىْ عَلَّمَ بِالْقَلَمِ ۙ ﴿٤﴾
عَلَّمَ الْاِنْسَانَ مَا لَمْ يَعْلَمْ ؕ كَلَّا اِنَّ الْاِنْسَانَ لَيَطْغٰى ۙ ﴿٦﴾ اَنْ رَّاٰهُ اسْتَغْنٰى ؕ ﴿٧﴾ اِنَّ اِلٰى رَبِّكَ الرُّجْعٰى ؕ
اَرَءَيْتَ الَّذِىْ يَنْهٰى ۙ ﴿٩﴾ عَبْدًا اِذَا صَلّٰى ؕ ﴿١٠﴾ اَرَءَيْتَ اِنْ كَانَ عَلَى الْهُدٰى ۙ
﴿١١﴾ اَوْ اَمَرَ بِالتَّقْوٰى ؕ ﴿١٢﴾ اَرَءَيْتَ اِنْ كَذَّبَ وَ تَوَلّٰى ؕ ﴿١٣﴾ اَلَمْ يَعْلَمْ بِاَنَّ اللّٰهَ يَرٰى ؕ

Read out to them [O Prophet] in the name of your Lord Who has created man from a clot of congealed blood. Read out to them, and in reality, your Lord is the most Bounteous who taught this Quran by the pen. He gave human beings in it that knowledge which he knew not. [Whatever frivolous talk they indulge in against it is baseless, O Prophet!] By no means! Man is surely being rebellious as he has considered himself self-sufficient. Undoubtedly, to your Lord will he [one day] have to return. Have you seen him who forbids a servant [of God] when he offers the prayer? Just consider if this servant happens to be on the right path or urges [others] to piety, … ? Just see if this [wretched] is the one who has denied and turned away, … ? Did he not know that God is watching? (Surah Alaq)

- The subject matter of the verses above makes it very clear that here the word Al-Insaan is used in two ways:
    - The first one is more general, where God is talking about the birth process.
    - The second one is more specific to people who are the direct addressees of the Quran
- Although they seem to have two distinct uses of the word Al-Insaan, they are pretty closely related.
- The second appearance of Al-Insaan refers to specific people among the addressees who were not only rejecting the message of the Quran but also becoming adversaries of the messenger and the Muslims.
- These people were reminded, through the initial verses, of their state of affairs when they came into this world and of the great blessing of the Quran bestowed upon them.
- They were stopping the Messenger and common Muslims from practicing their religion and started persecuting them. It is a sad situation that they are consequently opposing the God who has been generous to them throughout their lives, starting from their birth.
- Many interpreters of the Quran suggest that God is referring to Abu Jahl in these verses when He used the word Al-Insaan the second time. The style also suggests that God is talking about one person here.

Specific group in history – Example 1

لَآ أُقْسِمُ بِهَٰذَا الْبَلَدِ ﴿١﴾ وَ أَنتَ حِلٌّ بِهَٰذَا الْبَلَدِ ﴿٢﴾ وَ وَالِدٍ وَّ مَا وَلَدَ ﴿٣﴾ لَقَدْ خَلَقْنَا الْإِنسَانَ فِى كَبَدٍ ﴿٤﴾
أَيَحْسَبُ أَن لَّن يَقْدِرَ عَلَيْهِ أَحَدٌ ﴿٥﴾ يَقُولُ أَهْلَكْتُ مَالًا لُّبَدًا ﴿٦﴾ أَيَحْسَبُ أَن لَّمْ يَرَهُ أَحَدٌ ﴿٧﴾

No, [they were never always like this]! I call to witness this city [O Prophet!] [and this city is not alien to you;] you are its inhabitant and the father (Prophet Ibrahim) and his progeny also [who populated this city] that when We created man (nation of Ismail) here, he was surely in great toil at that time [due to barren land and difficult situation]. [Now that he is leading a life of affluence,] does he think that no one has power over him? [When he is asked to spend,] he says: "I have thrown away a lot of wealth." Does he think that no one has seen him? (Surah Balad: 1-7)

- God began this surah with an oath, referring to the birth of the nation of Prophet Muhammad thousands of years ago in this blessed city of Makkah, with Prophet Ibrahim, who settled his family here as instructed by God.
- Here, the word Al-Insaan refers to the nation born on this land for a mission from God.
- This was according to the greater plan of God in which He instructed Prophet Ibrahim to settle one of his wives with Prophet Ishaaq in the land of Palestine and another wife with Prophet Ismael in the land of Makkah, where the Kabaah was built.
- They start their lives in difficulty because of barren land and a lack of social fabric that makes any society flourish. The start of the Surah and the mention of the city and its earlier challenges were simply to compare their situation between now and then.
- Then God spoke about the behavior of disbelievers who have been enjoying God's blessings, because He made people attracted to the city of Makkah out of His Mercy and His plan to make it a center of worship for all human beings.
- In the subsequent verses, the singular pronoun "he" directly refers back to Al-Insaan; that's why the meaning narrows to a specific group of arrogant, wealthy leaders in Makkah who were actively opposing Prophet Muhammad.
- Earlier interpreters of the Quran took it as a universal human condition at the time of their birth. According to them, every person ever born enters a life of continuous struggle, labor, and testing.

Example 2

وَ التِّينِ وَ الزَّيْتُونِ ﴿١﴾ وَ طُورِ سِينِينَ ﴿٢﴾ وَ هٰذَا الْبَلَدِ الْأَمِينِ ﴿٣﴾ لَقَدْ خَلَقْنَا الْإِنْسَانَ فِي اَحْسَنِ تَقْوِيمٍ ﴿٤﴾
ثُمَّ رَدَدْنَاهُ اَسْفَلَ سَافِلِينَ ﴿٥﴾ اِلَّا الَّذِينَ اٰمَنُوا وَ عَمِلُوا الصَّالِحَاتِ فَلَهُمْ اَجْرٌ غَيْرُ مَمْنُونٍ

The mountains of Fig and Olive bear witness, and the mount of Sinai, and this secure city of yours, too, that when We created these [nations] [in these places], he was in the best of formation at that time. Then We reverted him to a low state when he himself wanted to become low. As for those who adhered to faith and did righteous deeds, for them shall be a reward unending. (Surah At-Teen: 1-6)

- This is a unique Surah that describes the entire history of three great Prophets and nations (two in the beginning) in a few sentences and identifies who will be successful in these nations.
- God took three oaths at the start of this Surah:
  - The mountains of fig and olive – this is the place where Jesus and the nation that called themselves Christian were born
  - Mount Sinai – where the nation of Moses was born because God took an oath with the Children of Israel here, and they were given Torah also
  - The safe and secure city of Makkah – where the nation of Ibrahim was born
- These three nations exist today. It all started with Prophet Ibrahim as one nation, but Judaism and Christianity took their own paths, developing distinct identities after the death of their Prophets.
- God told the believers and the disbelievers of the time to look at the history of these three nations.
- At the time of birth (when Messengers were given the responsibility), they were given the best guidance and the best people in the form of the Messengers.
- They were formed to lead other nations of the world. They had the best people among them.
- But then, due to their division, arrogance, and deviation from the message, they became the worst of the worst, which was a form of punishment for them from God.
- The only exceptions among the nations were those who truly believed in their messengers and remained steadfast in their righteous behavior, and they were saved from that state of disgrace in this life and in the Hereafter.
- This happened because of a special law that God prescribed for the Children of Israel and Ismael. According to this law, when the nation betrays the trust of the messenger and God, it is punished either by the best among them or by other nations.

Example 3

وَ الْعَصْرِ ﴿١﴾ اِنَّ الْاِنْسَانَ لَفِىْ خُسْرٍ ﴿٢﴾ اِلَّا الَّذِيْنَ اٰمَنُوْا وَ عَمِلُوا الصّٰلِحٰتِ وَ تَوَاصَوْا بِالْحَقِّ ۙ وَ تَوَاصَوْا بِالصَّبْرِ ﴿٣﴾

Time bears witness that these people shall definitely be in a state of loss. Yes, except those who professed faith, did righteous deeds, and urged one another to the truth, and urged one another to remain steadfast on the truth. (Surah Asr: 1-4)

- Many interpreters of the Quran have taken the word Al-Insaan to be generic. However, the *alif lam* affixed to it defines it, and the reference is to the nations of the Prophets and Messengers. For example, the nation of Prophet Ibrahim, who was settled in Makkah.
- The 'time' here refers to the complete history of Prophethood from the time of Adam.
- Loss here refers to loss both in this world and the next. In other words, they will be punished in this world like the other foremost addressees of other messengers of God were, and a great torment awaits them in the Hereafter.
- They have their eyes fixed on high status, power, and the wealth of this world. They think that opposing the Prophet is earning them a lucrative deal. In reality, they are facing the law of retribution and will soon reach their fate. Hence, they should remain aware that if they persist with this attitude, they will ultimately lose.
- In the coming verse, it is categorically stated how a person can secure himself from this loss.
    - Firm belief in God
    - Righteous deeds as a result of that belief
    - Counseling others and taking advice about the Truth
    - Continue to remain patient in the path of the Truth
- However, it is important to note that although the Quran specifically addressed a group of people who were blessed with the presence of messengers and prophets, the criteria for success still apply to us today.
- Some scholars argue that the Quran has provided the recipe for success in the Hereafter while we live our daily lives.
- It is common to observe that when we adhere to something because God wants us to, we face all kinds of challenges that require patience and mutual counseling.

Human beings in general – the creation

وَ لَقَدْ خَلَقْنَا الْإِنْسَانَ مِنْ سُلَالَةٍ مِّنْ طِينٍ * ثُمَّ جَعَلْنَهُ نُطْفَةً فِى قَرَارٍ مَّكِينٍ

[If those who deny you do not believe in this, then they should see:] We had created man from the essence of clay. Then, [subsequently] We made it through a drop of fluid and placed it in a secure spot. (Surah Mu'minun: 12-13)

وَ لَقَدْ خَلَقْنَا الْإِنْسَانَ مِنْ صَلْصَالٍ مِّنْ حَمَإٍ مَّسْنُونٍ

[These are the people who have been lured by Iblis. Remind them that] We had created man with stinking mud that rings (Surah Hijr: 26)

إِنَّا خَلَقْنَا الْإِنْسَانَ مِنْ نُطْفَةٍ أَمْشَاجٍ * نَّبْتَلِيهِ فَجَعَلْنَهُ سَمِيعًا بَصِيرًا

In reality, We have created man from a drop of mingled fluid. Then We continued to let it go through multiple phases until made him capable of hearing and seeing (the capacity to process through these two faculties). (Surah Insaan: 2)

- All these verses are self-explanatory, in which God speaks about human beings at the time of their creation and birth. Here, Al-Insaan refers to human beings in general.

THE QURAN ON HUMAN EVOLUTION

- When the Quran uses terms such as the essence of clay, stinking mud, or clay that rings, it describes the first phase of human evolution, during which the physical/animal form of man was created.
- For this, the same process of creation that is now carried out in the mother's womb was then carried out in the earth's belly.
- Thus, soil components that enter our bodies as food and therein transform into gametes to initiate the process of human production underwent the same process in the mud of a riverbank or seashore to produce the first life-germ.
- The mud surrounding this life-germ, or cell, dried up and formed an egg-like shell around it, which the Quran alludes to as 'sounding clay'.
- Within such an egg-like lodging, the various stages of prenatal development were accomplished. Eventually, a fully formed creature hatched out, capable of looking after itself. This creature should be called the animal form of man.
- The animal form of man was further refined, perhaps through breeding of many generations, until it became capable of receiving the human soul and the capability of understanding through hearing, seeing, and pondering. The Quran describes these phases in Surah Sajdah (7-9).

Human beings in general – Ungrateful

اَللّٰهُ الَّذِیْ خَلَقَ السَّمٰوٰتِ وَ الْاَرْضَ وَ اَنْزَلَ مِنَ السَّمَآءِ مَآءً فَاَخْرَجَ بِهٖ مِنَ الثَّمَرٰتِ رِزْقًا لَّكُمْ ۚ وَ سَخَّرَ لَكُمُ الْفُلْكَ لِتَجْرِیَ فِی الْبَحْرِ بِاَمْرِهٖ ۚ وَ سَخَّرَ لَكُمُ الْاَنْهٰرَ ۝۳۲ وَ سَخَّرَ لَكُمُ الشَّمْسَ وَ الْقَمَرَ دَآئِبَیْنِ ۚ وَ سَخَّرَ لَكُمُ الَّیْلَ وَ النَّهَارَ ۝۳۳ وَ اٰتٰىكُمْ مِّنْ كُلِّ مَا سَاَلْتُمُوْهُ ۚ وَ اِنْ تَعُدُّوْا نِعْمَتَ اللّٰهِ لَا تُحْصُوْهَا ۚ اِنَّ الْاِنْسَانَ لَظَلُوْمٌ كَفَّارٌ ۝۳۴

[Do these Idolaters not see that] it is God Who created the heavens and the earth and sent down water from the sky. Then through it produced various fruits for your sustenance and put the ship to your service that it may sail in the sea at His behest, and He put the seas to your service and the sun and the moon also; both are moving continuously. Similarly, day and night, He puts to your service and has given you everything you asked for. If you dare to count the favors of God, you will never be able to count them. [Even then, you associate partners with Him?] In reality, man is very unjust and very ungrateful. (Surah Ibrahim: 32-34)

- The address is to the man as a human being. God, according to His wisdom and purpose, has bestowed upon you everything you were made dependent upon by your very nature and creation.

- This perfect correspondence between human need (and other creatures' needs) and its fulfillment is itself the greatest evidence that the One who created you is the same One who provided for all your needs.

- Though the word 'man' here is general, at the same time, its discourse is primarily directed toward those polytheists mentioned in the preceding verse. Since they are unworthy of direct attention because of their unfitness, the statement is made in general terms.

- 'Zalum' (Injustice) means one who usurps rights. By committing shirk (polytheism), or even rejecting the existence of God, man usurps the rights of God as well as the rights of his own soul. 'Kaffar' means ungrateful—one who receives blessings from one source but sings the praises of another one or remains ungrateful to the Giver, considering the blessing as their right.

Evolutionary Biologists' Viewpoint on Universe Serving Us

- The Earth wasn't custom-made to fit us, as we believe, but rather, we were shaped by the Earth.

- Over billions of years, living organisms that possessed traits poorly suited to their environment did not survive or pass on their genes. Only the plants and animals with variations that allowed them to successfully breathe the available air, drink the water, and eat the food survived to reproduce.

- This means life adapts to the planet's existing conditions through natural selection, making it look like the Earth has everything perfectly prepared for us, when in reality, we are just the specialized puzzle pieces that evolved to fit the shape of the world around us

Human beings are generally ungrateful

- In the Quran, the concept of human ingratitude is framed as a fundamental challenge to their character. While God has bestowed immeasurable blessings upon humanity, the "default" human state, when left without reminders, is one of forgetfulness and complaining.

- The scholars of the Quran emphasize a profound linguistic connection between ingratitude (absence of Shukr) and disbelief (Kufr).

- Just as a farmer covers a seed with soil, an ungrateful person "covers up" God's favors by refusing to acknowledge them or by attributing their success solely to their own efforts.

- The ungratefulness does not allow a sense of contentment to settle within us. It's a constant battle for me.

- On the other hand, Shukr not only helps build the lover for the Creator but also instills appreciation and cooperation between people and brings about a profound change in us as individuals.

Human Psychology

- Hedonic Adaptation: Also known as the "hedonic treadmill," this is the tendency for humans to quickly return to a stable level of happiness despite major positive changes. What was once a "blessing" (like a new job or home) becomes the "new normal," causing the initial gratitude to fade.

- Research by psychologists like **Robert Emmons** suggests that a sense of entitlement—the belief that one *deserves* certain benefits—is the "enemy of gratitude." When we feel entitled, we view gifts as obligations or rights, leaving no room for thankfulness.

Example 2 – Despair Fast

لَا يَسْأَمُ الْإِنْسَانُ مِنْ دُعَاءِ الْخَيْرِ ۖ وَ إِنْ مَّسَّهُ الشَّرُّ فَيَئُوسٌ قَنُوطٌ ﴿٤٩﴾ وَ لَئِنْ أَذَقْنَاهُ رَحْمَةً مِّنَّا مِنْ بَعْدِ ضَرَّآءَ مَسَّتْهُ لَيَقُولَنَّ هَٰذَا لِي

[Strange is the matter of] Man, when hardships come his way, he does not get tired of supplicating for goodness, but if he is faced with a calamity and sees that his supplications are not being answered, he loses hope and despairs. And, if after that calamity which has afflicted him, We make him taste Our mercy, he says: "This is only my right". (Haa Meem Sajdah: 49-50)

- God said that if a person attains blessings and prosperity, instead of being grateful to Him, he thinks he is entitled to them and that they happened because of his efforts.
- Yet, if he falls slightly into God's grasp, he offers long, repetitive prayers to escape it, vowing that if he is delivered from this grip, he will forever remain His grateful and obedient servant.
- But this is merely a deception, and what he is saying is not true. When God rescues him from that calamity, he indulges himself again in the same heedless pleasures in which he was previously engrossed.
- And if God does not grant him relief from that trouble, or if the hardship is prolonged, instead of remaining content and patient with God's decree, he becomes utterly broken-hearted, discouraged, and loses hope in God.
- They despair quickly in such circumstances and usually ask questions like, "O God, why me?"
- Such individuals are very active in praying for their worldly success and progress. To them, 'praying for good' (dua-e-khair) means only praying for worldly advancement. However, this is contrary to common experience and observation. As long as their ship is sailing smoothly, such people never turn toward God; rather, they remain absorbed in their own ambitions and lost in their desires.

Example 3 - Hasty

اِنَّ الْاِنْسَانَ خُلِقَ هَلُوْعًا ﴿١٩﴾ اِذَا مَسَّهُ الشَّرُّ جَزُوْعًا ﴿٢٠﴾ وَّ اِذَا مَسَّهُ الْخَيْرُ مَنُوْعًا

[These people shall continue asking you to hasten the punishment. Just ignore them.] In reality, man has been created very impatient (anxious). Whenever some affliction befalls him, he becomes impatient, and when good fortune befalls him, he becomes very stingy. (Surah Maarij:19-21)

خُلِقَ الْاِنْسَانُ مِنْ عَجَلٍ ۚ سَاُورِيْكُمْ اٰيٰتِيْ فَلَا تَسْتَعْجِلُوْنِ

[They want to hasten the torment. In reality,] man is made of the essence of impatience (referring to his nature). I shall soon show you My signs. So, do not be hasty (for my decisions) (Surah Anbiya:37)

- Classical scholars such as Ibn Kathir and Al-Qurtubi note that the Quran itself immediately defines the word بَلُوغًا in the two verses that follow this verse.

- When evil touches him, he is desperate/fretful (جَزُوعًا). When good touches him, he is withholding/stingy (مَنُوعًا).

- This specific trait manifests directly as the behavioral pattern of alternating between panic and entitlement.

- Scholars clarify that being created with these raw tendencies is a deliberate part of the worldly test, not an inherent defect.

- The base human template is intentionally given an "accelerator" (passions, haste, and fear) so that humans can earn spiritual merit by actively developing their "brakes" (self-control, patience, and trust in God). Man is punished or rewarded based on the conscious choices made through free will, not for possessing the raw emotional canvas.

- The Quran never leaves a negative diagnosis without a remedy. Verse 22 immediately (after the above verse) provides the structural exception to this natural human volatility. The verses after these discuss the characteristics of believers who take control of these raw tendencies.

Example 4 – Self-aware but heedless

يَقُولُ الْإِنْسَانُ يَوْمَئِذٍ أَيْنَ الْمَفَرُّ ﴿١٠﴾ كَلَّا لَا وَزَرَ ﴿١١﴾ إِلَى رَبِّكَ يَوْمَئِذٍ الْمُسْتَقَرُّ ﴿١٢﴾ يُنَبَّؤُا الْإِنْسَانُ يَوْمَئِذٍ بِمَا قَدَّمَ وَ أَخَّرَ ﴿١٣﴾ بَلِ الْإِنْسَانُ عَلَى نَفْسِهِ بَصِيرَةٌ ﴿١٤﴾ وَ لَوْ أَلْقَى مَعَاذِيرَهُ

The human beings will say on that day: "Where to flee?" No way! There is no refuge now! On that day, you will only rest once in front of your Lord. On that day, man will be informed what he has sent forth and what he has left behind. In fact, the truth is that man himself is a witness upon his own self (own deeds), however much he may put up excuses for himself. (Surah Qiyamah:10-15)

- These verses address another attribute of human beings, especially when they commit wrong but are not ready to acknowledge it and even justify it. They are self-aware of their actions.

- People do commit mischief in the presence of their conscience and self-reproaching souls, completely disregarding their reminders and warnings.

- The greatest evidence of the Day of Resurrection exists right within man's own soul, but what remedy is there for a person who stands up to contradict and deny his own self!

- God stated here that man's conscience alone is sufficient to establish proof of the Resurrection; however, the mouth of a person who is determined to have the audacity to 'lie right to your face' cannot be shut.
- From this, it also follows that whoever commits an evil deed against his self-reproaching soul—or in other words, against his conscience—is in reality committing that evil in the presence of God. This is because the conscience is actually a censor and judge appointed by God; so, whoever commits evil before it has, in fact, committed evil before God Himself.

Example 5 – Crisis 'believer'

رَبُّكُمُ الَّذِى يُزْجِىْ لَكُمُ الْفُلْكَ فِى الْبَحْرِ لِتَبْتَغُوْا مِنْ فَضْلِهٖ ؕ اِنَّهٗ كَانَ بِكُمْ رَحِيْمًا ﴿٦٦﴾ وَ اِذَا مَسَّكُمُ الضُّرُّ فِى الْبَحْرِ ضَلَّ مَنْ تَدْعُوْنَ اِلَّاۤ اِيَّاهُ ۚ فَلَمَّا نَجّٰكُمْ اِلَى الْبَرِّ اَعْرَضْتُمْ ؕ وَ كَانَ الْاِنْسَانُ كَفُوْرًا

[People!] Your Lord is one who makes the ship sail for you in the sea so that you can seek His bounty. Undoubtedly, He is very Merciful to you. When you are struck by a calamity in the sea, all those you invoke besides Him are forgotten; only He is remembered. Then, when He safely brings you to the shore, you turn away. In reality, man is very ungrateful. (Surah Bani Israel: 66-67)

وَ اِذَا مَسَّ الْاِنْسَانَ ضُرٌّ دَعَا رَبَّهٗ مُنِيْبًا اِلَيْهِ ثُمَّ اِذَا خَوَّلَهٗ نِعْمَةً مِّنْهُ نَسِىَ مَا كَانَ يَدْعُوْۤا اِلَيْهِ مِنْ قَبْلُ وَ جَعَلَ لِلّٰهِ اَنْدَادًا لِّيُضِلَّ عَنْ سَبِيْلِهٖ ؕ قُلْ تَمَتَّعْ بِكُفْرِكَ قَلِيْلًا ۖ اِنَّكَ مِنْ اَصْحٰبِ النَّارِ

[Strange is the case of human beings.] When some calamity strikes man, he calls God while turning towards Him. Then, when his Lord grants Him some favor from Himself, he forgets that for which he was pleading earlier and starts associating partners with God to lead people away from His path. Tell him [O Prophet!]: Enjoy for some days with this disbelief of yours; there is no doubt that one day you shall ultimately be among the companions of Hell. (Surah Zumr: 8)

- In these verses, God described the situation of the Prophet's addressees, using a parable about human behavior.
- This is a parable illustrating that every blessing a person receives comes solely from Allah Almighty. It is due to Him that man should enjoy this blessing while remaining deeply grateful to his Lord.
- However, it is a strange misfortune of man that when he receives a blessing, he becomes arrogant toward God, attributing everything to the miracle of his own effort and planning, or to the grace and benevolence of his presumed gods and goddesses.

- Yet, the moment he faces adversity, he begins to call out to God desperately, completely forgetting all those gods and goddesses (which could be his desires) at that time. Then, once Allah rescues him from that adversity, his past intoxication of neglect returns to him, and he shelves God away in the cabinet of oblivion once again.

- To clarify this reality, the example of traveling by boat on a river is given. It is solely due to God's power that a ship weighing thousands of tons moves across the chest of the ocean. God established this system so that mankind could benefit from it in their travels and remain grateful for God's grace and mercy.

- But man's condition is such that as long as the boat sails smoothly, the thought of God never even crosses his mind. However, when the boat gets caught in a storm and begins to rock violently, he completely forgets both his arrogance and his indifference to God. At that moment, he cries out and appeals to God alone for help. Yet, this state only lasts as long as the boat remains trapped in that whirlpool of calamity.

- The very moment the boat escapes that whirlpool and man sets foot on dry land, he no longer remembers that hour of distress, nor does he recall his weeping and beseeching before God.

Assignment

Find a few verses in the Quran with the word Al-Insaan and determine from the context which group the address belongs to.

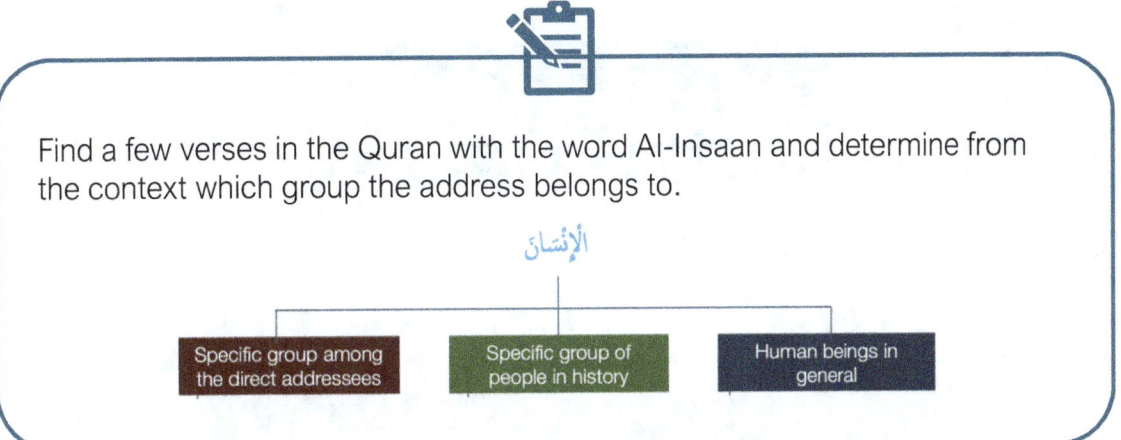

Chapter 18

Studying Surah Al-Fatihah

In this chapter, we will study Surah Fatihah by applying the principles of understanding the Quran we have studied in this course.

Placement of Surah Al-Fatihah

Chapter 1: 1, 2, 3, 4, 5
Chapter 2: 6, 7, 8, 9
Chapter 3: 10, 11, 12, 13, 14, 15, 16, 17, 18, 19, 20, 21, 22, 23, 24
Chapter 4: 25, 26, 27, 28, 29, 30, 31, 32, 33
Chapter 5: 34, 35, 36, 37, 38, 39, 40, 41, 42, 43, 44, 45, 46, 47, 48, 49
Chapter 6: 50, 51, 52, 53, 54, 55, 56, 57, 58, 59, 60, 61, 62, 63, 64, 65, 66
Chapter 7: 67, 68, 69, 70, 71, 72, 73, 74, 75, 76, 77, 78, 79, 80, 81, 82, 83, 84, 85,
86, 87, 88, 89, 90, 91, 92, 93, 94, 95, 96, 97, 98, 99, 100, 101, 102, 103, 104, 105,
106, 107, 108, 109, 110, 111, 112, 113, 114

Commissioning	1
Specific Warning	6
General Warning	37
Completion of Arguments	31
Migration and Cutting Ties	16
Purification and selection	15
Reward and Punishment	2

Medani Surahs

- It's a Makkan Surah.
- It is the first Surah of the Quran.
- It is part of Chapter 1 of the Quran, one of its seven chapters.
- It belongs to a very special phase of the Prophet Muhammad's mission, known as the **Commissioning** phase.
- This is the phase when Prophet Muhammad was appointed as the Messenger of God on earth.

The nature of Surah Al-Fatihah

Humanity made Dua
O Allah, Guide us to the straight path

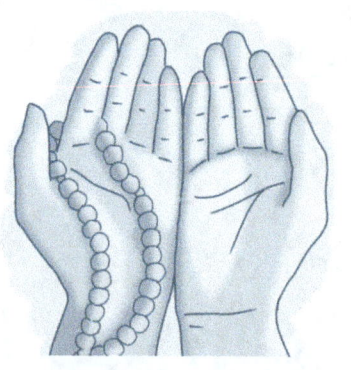

Allah answered the call

The Quran

- With regard to its subject matter, this surah is a supplication to seek guidance from the Almighty for the straight path – a prayer which was the wish of every upright person during the time of the Prophet Muhammad. After the Jews and the Christians had distorted the face of religion through their innovations and deviations, it was, in fact, the desire of every heart to receive fresh guidance. The Almighty articulated this desire through the tongue of His Prophet in these eternal and matchless words.

- This prayer for fresh guidance after the Torah and the Injil is also the central theme of this surah. Consequently, its relationship with the Madinan surahs of the first group is characterized by brevity and detail, as mentioned in the introduction to the group. However, from a subject-matter perspective, it serves as an appropriate preface to the Quran as well.

- Viewed thus, it is evident that this is the first complete surah revealed to the Prophet Muhammad in Makkah.

- That's why in Salah, it is mandatory to recite Surah Fatihah and some part of the Quran to ascertain the relationship between Surah Fatihah and the rest of the Quran.

- This Surah also teaches us the etiquette of making dua. Every dua must start with praising Allah first before asking for anything. Also, the best thing a Muslim can ask for is guidance on the path of Allah.

> Many Scholars agree that Surah Al-Fatiha is the First Complete Surah of the Quran revealed to Prophet Muhammad due to its subject

Surah Al-Fatihah & Its Importance

بِسْمِ اللَّهِ الرَّحْمَنِ الرَّحِيمِ

الْحَمْدُ لِلَّهِ رَبِّ الْعَالَمِينَ   الرَّحْمَنِ الرَّحِيمِ   مَالِكِ يَوْمِ الدِّينِ

إِيَّاكَ نَعْبُدُ وَإِيَّاكَ نَسْتَعِينُ   اهْدِنَا الصِّرَاطَ الْمُسْتَقِيمَ

صِرَاطَ الَّذِينَ أَنْعَمْتَ عَلَيْهِمْ غَيْرِ الْمَغْضُوبِ   عَلَيْهِمْ وَلاَ الضَّالِّينَ

In the name of Allah (on the Authority of), the Most Gracious, the Ever Merciful. Gratitude is for God only, the Lord of the universe. The Most Gracious, the Ever-Merciful. The Master of the Day of Judgement. [Lord] You alone we worship, and only Your help we seek. Bestow on us the guidance of the straight path— the path of those you have blessed who have neither earned your wrath nor have gone astray.

- The first three verses after Bismillah praise God.
- The next three verses are the actual dua.
- This is such a powerful dua that the Prophet made it mandatory for us to recite it in every unit of Salah. At a minimum, every Muslim recites this dua 17 times a day.
- Surah Fatihah is mandatory for the Salah unit to be considered complete. Prophet Muhammad once said, No Salah without Fatihah.

The Basmala

Ba: When the Prophet says this, he isn't speaking by himself but with the Authority of Allah.

بِسْمِ اللَّهِ الرَّحْمَنِ الرَّحِيمِ

Message from the King of the Universe

- This verse occurs at the start of every Surah except Surah Tawbah.
- It is a verse of the Quran, but not a part of any Surah.
- It has an independent status in all these places.
- It implies: "**O Prophet, read out this Surah to the people from ME.**"
- In Surah Alaq, it is used in a similar way in the following verse:

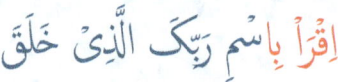

اِقْرَأْ بِاسْمِ رَبِّكَ الَّذِى خَلَقَ

Read out to them [O Prophet] in the name of your Lord Who has created (Surah Alaq:1)

- The particle 'ب' indicates authority, and the verse manifests a prediction made in the Old Testament regarding Prophet Muhammad.
- According to this prediction, God said in Old Testmament:

"I will raise among them a prophet like you (O Moses) from among their brothers; I will put My words in his mouth, and he will tell them everything I command him. If anyone does not listen to My words that the prophet speaks in My name, I will call him to account. (Deuteronomy, 18:18)

The concept of thanks to Allah

الْحَمْدُ لِلَّهِ رَبِّ الْعَالَمِينَ

Allah: AL+ILAH, which means "The God." Arabs knew this name before Prophet Muhammad. The Quran used the same name as the Arabs.

Al Hamd: This word is used to acknowledge the greatness and favors of someone. If the person who expresses this word is also benefiting from the said favors, the element of gratitude automatically enters the word's meaning. It is evident from 7:42, 10:10, and 14:39 that the word is used to connote gratitude in the expression. The use of *Alif-Laam* here is to cover all forms of praise and gratitude.

Rabb: The word Rabb contains three aspects

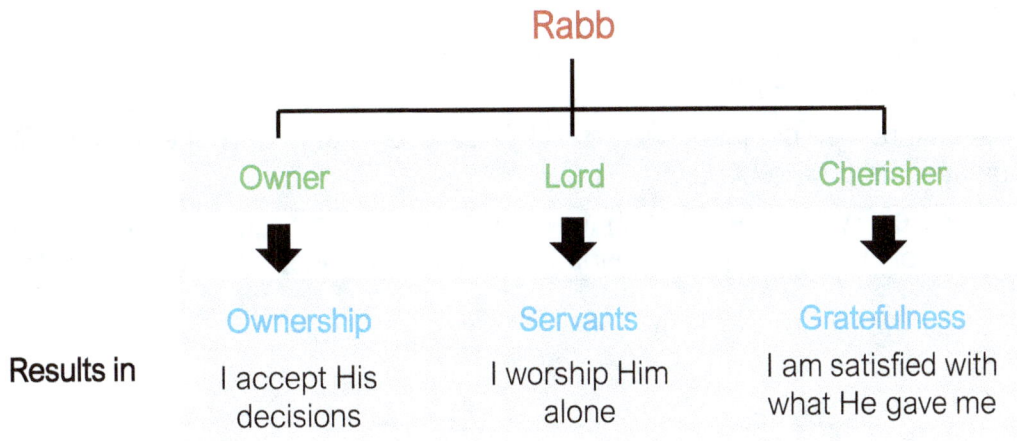

	Owner	Lord	Cherisher
	↓	↓	↓
	Ownership	Servants	Gratefulness
Results in	I accept His decisions	I worship Him alone	I am satisfied with what He gave me

Find a few verses in the Quran where Allah mentions various human attitudes and reactions in this life for them to ponder and self-reflect.

Mercy in all forms

- The word Rahman is in the intensive form, expressing great fervency and enthusiasm. It means the type of Mercy that wants to manifest itself.
- The word Rahman also conveys the concept of Justice, including punishment and reward. The Day of Judgment is the result of this Mercy. Anyone who is Merciful would not allow criminals to do whatever they want.
- Similarly, anyone who is Merciful would not leave the people without compensating them if they have been wronged.
- The word Raheem expresses steadiness and permanence (always).
- The enthusiasm and warmth of Mercy are complemented by a sense of permanence.
- Both are needed to be Merciful.
- Examples:
  - He was Merciful and created this universe, arranging everything needed to sustain us on this Earth.
  - He made human beings the rulers of this Earth and then gave them constant guidance on how to behave.
  - He gave everyone free will so that people can act freely in this world, but then He will hold unjust people accountable for their injustices against God or others.

يَٰٓأَبَتِ إِنِّىٓ أَخَافُ أَن يَمَسَّكَ عَذَابٌ مِّنَ الرَّحْمَٰنِ فَتَكُونَ لِلشَّيْطَٰنِ وَلِيًّا

Dear Father! I fear that some torment of the **Most Gracious God may seize you,** and you end up becoming the companion of Satan. (19:45)

يَوْمَ نَحْشُرُ الْمُتَّقِينَ إِلَى الرَّحْمَٰنِ وَفْدًا وَّ نَسُوقُ الْمُجْرِمِينَ إِلَىٰ جَهَنَّمَ وِرْدًا

لَا يَمْلِكُونَ الشَّفَاعَةَ إِلَّا مَنِ اتَّخَذَ عِندَ الرَّحْمَٰنِ عَهْدًا

Remind them that We shall bring together the pious towards the **Merciful God** as guests and drive the wrongdoers towards Hell, thirsty. On that day, they will not have the authority to bring any intercession except he who has taken a promise from the **Merciful God**. (19:85-87)

Mercy demands Justice

Ad-Deen: The day when people will be rewarded مَالِكِ يَوْمِ الدِّينِ

- As a result of His Mercy, He would set up His court of justice.
- He would be the Supreme Authority; everyone would bow to Him in total submission.
- He would then decide all cases by Himself, and no one could influence His decisions in any manner.
- Complete negation of any thoughts that on that Day anyone would be able to save us – even the Prophets will be allowed to talk after the permission is given.

قُلْ لِّمَنْ مَّا فِى السَّمٰوٰتِ وَ الْأَرْضِ ۗ قُلْ لِّلّٰهِ ۚ كَتَبَ عَلٰى نَفْسِهِ الرَّحْمَةَ ۚ لَيَجْمَعَنَّكُمْ اِلٰى يَوْمِ الْقِيٰمَةِ لَا رَيْبَ فِيهِ

Ask them: To whom belongs all that is in the heavens and the earth? Say: To God alone. He has made mercy mandatory on Himself. (That's why) He shall definitely gather all of you to the Day of Judgement about which there is no doubt. (6:12)

- *Yaum Ad-Deen*: The literal meaning of this statement is the Day of Transactions. The Day of Judgment will be the day of transactions because on that day, God will exchange reward and punishment against deeds. Also, on that day, people's deeds will be exchanged if someone has wronged another.

اِنَّمَا تُوْعَدُوْنَ لَصَادِقٌ ۙ وَّاِنَّ الدِّيْنَ لَوَاقِعٌ

[They bear witness] that the scourge you are being threatened with is undeniably certain, and reward and punishment are bound to take place. (51:5-6)

Surah Al-Fatihah encompasses the simple message of Islam

LORD ➡ MERCIFUL ➡ MASTER

- Allah, the Creator, is our Lord, the Cherisher and Sustainer who deserves our worship and gratitude.

- Because of His Infinite Mercy He would establish the Court of Justice.

- He will be the Master of that day alone, so be prepared for accountability.

The core message of Islam is straightforward and revolves around three fundamental truths. The rest are the details:

- **Oneness of God (Tawhid):** God alone is the Creator and Sovereign. Associating partners with Him (shirk) is the gravest injustice, and tawhid acts as the boundary wall protecting all of religion.
- **Day of Judgement (Akhirah):** The world is not purposeless; it will culminate in a Day of Judgement. This belief flows naturally from recognizing God's wisdom, mercy, and justice. Denying it means denying His providence and fairness.
- **Accountability:** Human beings will be held accountable for their choices and deeds. The Quran repeatedly stresses that oppression, injustice, and ingratitude cannot go unchecked; ultimate justice will be served in the Hereafter.

اِنَّ الَّذِيْنَ اٰمَنُوْا وَ الَّذِيْنَ هَادُوْا وَ النَّصٰرٰى وَ الصّٰبِئِيْنَ مَنْ اٰمَنَ بِاللّٰهِ وَ الْيَوْمِ الْاٰخِرِ وَ عَمِلَ صَالِحًا فَلَهُمْ اَجْرُهُمْ عِنْدَ رَبِّهِمْ وَ لَا خَوْفٌ عَلَيْهِمْ وَ لَا هُمْ يَحْزَنُوْنَ

Those who have professed faith [in the unlettered Prophet] and those [before them] who became Jews and those who are called Nasara, and Sabaeans – whoever among them have believed in God and in the Last Day and have done righteous deeds – for them their reward lies with their Lord and [in His gracious presence] they shall have nothing to fear nor shall they ever grieve. (2:62)

Submission and Seeking Help

After understanding our relationship with Allah, this is the only possible statement to come to a person's tongue

 إِيَّاكَ نَعْبُدُ وَإِيَّاكَ نَسْتَعِينُ

- **Ibadah** is primarily used in Arabic to mean 'humility' and 'submission', much like a slave shows to his master.
- The Quran has used this word explicitly to describe a person's humility and servility in the presence of their Creator.
- The primary manifestation of these inner feelings is Worship (prayers and other forms)
- **"To you"** shows "it is only you" – the best way to negate polytheism.
- If Allah is our Lord, sustains everything, deserves our gratitude, and is the King on the Day of Judgement, it makes perfect sense to seek His help alone.
- No one besides Him can help.
- **Seeking help from Him** alone is another manifestation of submitting to Him.
- In most polytheistic religions, they claim they worship Allah, but they seek help from others, thinking Allah would listen to supplications due to the closeness of others to Allah.

If we must seek help from Allah alone, why do we ask for help from other human beings? Does it negate the concept of asking Him alone?

The Straight Path

Guide us <u>to</u> the straight path   اهْدِنَا الصِّرَاطَ الْمُسْتَقِيمَ

- The straight path is the easiest and generally the quickest way to reach a destination.
- Instead of telling us what the straight path is, He gave us examples of people we should follow and those we should avoid.
- But Satan promised Allah he would sit on the straight path and misguide people. Staying on it is the most difficult job now.
- Surah Baqarah and Aal-e-Imran show how Jews and Christians got misguided from the straight path.

The verb *IHDINA* should occur here with the preposition *ILA*. However, there is no ILA here. Suppression of this preposition adds emphasis to the meaning of the verb. This does not simply mean 'guide us to the straight path.' It means: **"Set our hearts on the straight path; give us the resolve, determination, and facility to stay on it."**

- The straight path begins with the sincere belief in the absolute oneness of God (Tawhid) and the devotion of all worship to Him alone. The Quran explicitly links worship with the straight path, as in the verse, *"Indeed, Allah is my Lord and your Lord, so worship Him. This is the straight path" (Qur'an 3:51).*
- The straight path is inseparable from God's revealed guidance in the Quran. The Quran itself is described as showing *"the straightest way" (Qur'an 17:9),* providing clarity and direction out of darkness into divine clarity.
- The straight path requires both correct belief and principled, obedient action.
- The path is defined by clarity and is free from the extremes and excessive complexities that people sometimes add to religion.
- Following the straight path means following in the footsteps of the prophets, including Abraham, Moses, and Jesus, who all called to the same path of worship and upright conduct.

Learn from the Examples

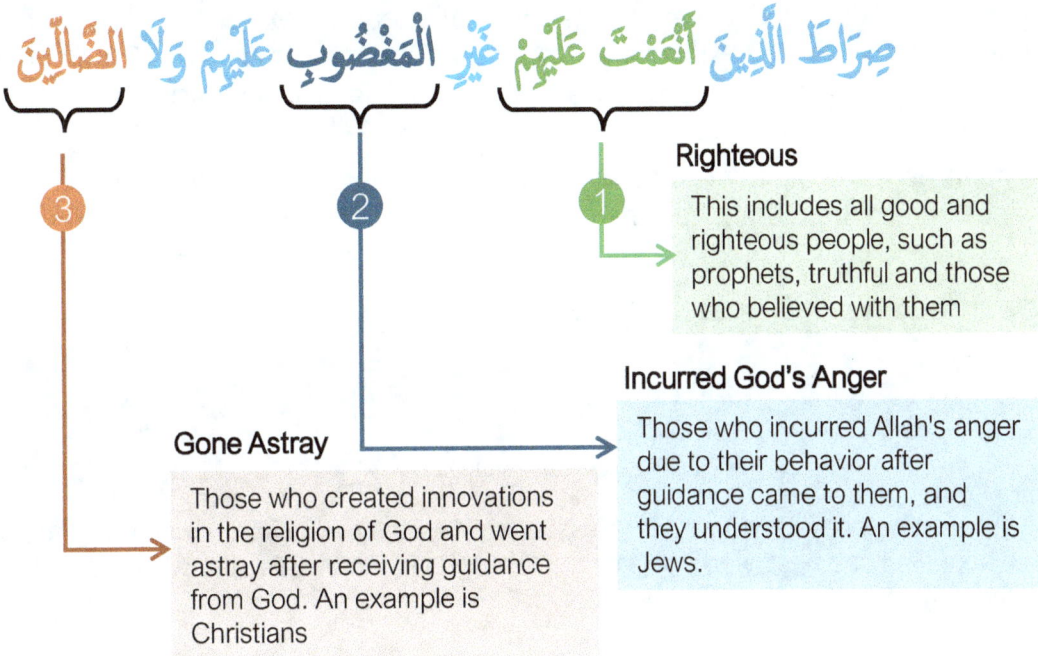

Righteous

This includes all good and righteous people, such as prophets, truthful and those who believed with them

Incurred God's Anger

Those who incurred Allah's anger due to their behavior after guidance came to them, and they understood it. An example is Jews.

Gone Astray

Those who created innovations in the religion of God and went astray after receiving guidance from God. An example is Christians

Shifts in the addressee in the Quran – Example

Verses 1-3
Gratitude is for God only, the Lord of the universe.
The Most Gracious, the Ever-Merciful.
The Master of the Day of Judgement.

Introduction to the person of God with no addressee

Verses 4-7
[Lord] You alone we worship, and only Your help we seek. Bestow on us the guidance of the straight path. The path of those you have blessed, who have neither earned your wrath nor gone astray.

Now, a believer seeking guidance suddenly directly addresses God.

Quran Explains Itself – Example

- Recall the principle that the Quran explains its own verses.
- Think of the Quran like a teacher who repeats the same lesson in different ways. If you don't understand it in math class when the teacher explains it with numbers, it later clicks when they explain it with a diagram or an example. The Quran does the same—it teaches its message by explaining itself in different parts, so you understand better.
- The three types of people God discussed in these last verses are explained elsewhere in the Quran. Let's review them.

Rewarded ones – Righteous Believers

وَ مَنْ يُّطِعِ اللهَ وَ الرَّسُوْلَ فَاُولٰٓئِكَ مَعَ الَّذِيْنَ اَنْعَمَ اللهُ عَلَيْهِمْ مِّنَ النَّبِيّٖنَ وَ الصِّدِّيْقِيْنَ وَ الشُّهَدَآءِ وَ الصّٰلِحِيْنَ

Those who obey God and His Messenger, it is they who shall dwell with those whom God has **bestowed with favor**: the prophets, the truthful, the witnesses, and the righteous (4:69)

Earned Anger – Jews

وَ ضُرِبَتْ عَلَيْهِمُ الذِّلَّةُ وَ الْمَسْكَنَةُ وَ بَآءُوْ بِغَضَبٍ مِّنَ اللهِ

Humiliation and misery were stamped upon them (the Children of Israel), and they earned the **wrath of God**. (2:61)

Gone Astray – Christians

قُلْ يَآ اَهْلَ الْكِتٰبِ لَا تَغْلُوْا فِيْ دِيْنِكُمْ غَيْرَ الْحَقِّ وَ لَا تَتَّبِعُوْٓا اَهْوَآءَ قَوْمٍ قَدْ ضَلُّوْا مِنْ قَبْلُ وَ اَضَلُّوْا كَثِيْرًا

Say: O People of the Book! Do not exaggerate in your religion without any basis, and do not follow the religious innovations of those people who had already been **led astray** and who led many others astray.

Muslims can fall under any of the groups depending on their attitude or behavior (1, 2 or 3). This is not specific to any group by race or religion.

Surah Al-Fatiha in our lives

- Allah wants us to start our prayers by saying, "All thanks and gratitude belong to Allah" under all circumstances. For example, imagine these situations just before a person is about to pray Zuhr prayers:
    - He/she got the best grades in the class – Saying AlhamduLillah in the prayers
    - He/she moved to a new house – Saying AlhamduLillah in the prayers
    - One of their loved ones died – Saying AlhamduLillah in the prayers
    - The doctor reports concluded that he/she has cancer – Saying AlhamduLillah in the prayers
- Surah Fatihah changes the way we view this world and our lives.
- He is our Lord, Owner, and Sustainer; He can do all of the above, and we cannot question.
- This universe is purposefully created for the test; we can never succeed without finding the recipe for passing it (the Straight Path).

Names of Allah coming together as a pair

God does not bring two names together in the Quran randomly but with great wisdom behind it. Some examples are presented here:

الْعَزِيزُ الْحَكِيمُ	The Most Powerful the Most Wise He is All-Powerful, but He uses His powers with great Wisdom
عَفُوٌّ غَفُورٌ	Pardoning and Forgiving He not only conceals sins (forgives) but can erase them (pardons) completely from our books if we deserve it
غَفُورٌ رَّحِيمٌ	Forgiving Ever Merciful He will only forgive those who deserve to be forgiven according to His attribute of Mercy
ٱلسَّمِيعُ ٱلْعَلِيمُ	All-Hearing All-Knowing He not only hears what's been said, but He understands fully the purpose and intention behind those words

The Quran is revealed for the entire humanity. Why is the nation of Bani Israel discussed so much in the Quran?

Assignment

In the Quran, Allah often mentions two of His attributes together at the end of the verses. One example in Surah Al-Fatihah was **Al-Rahman** and **Al-Raheem**. Identify three additional places in the Quran, each with a different name, to gain a deeper understanding of the meaning of each attribute and how they interact with one another. Use names other than those that have already been mentioned in the examples before.

Chapter 19

Studying Surah Al-Kauthar

In this chapter, we will study Surah Al-Kauthar by applying the principles of understanding the Quran we have studied in this course.

Placement of Surah Kauthar

Chapter 1: 1, 2, 3, 4, 5
Chapter 2: 6, 7, 8, 9
Chapter 3: 10, 11, 12, 13, 14, 15, 16, 17, 18, 19, 20, 21, 22, 23, 24
Chapter 4: 25, 26, 27, 28, 29, 30, 31, 32, 33
Chapter 5: 34, 35, 36, 37, 38, 39, 40, 41, 42, 43, 44, 45, 46, 47, 48, 49
Chapter 6: 50, 51, 52, 53, 54, 55, 56, 57, 58, 59, 60, 61, 62, 63, 64, 65, 66
Chapter 7: 67, 68, 69, 70, 71, 72, 73, 74, 75, 76, 77, 78, 79, 80, 81, 82, 83, 84, 85, 86, 87, 88, 89, 90, 91, 92, 93, 94, 95, 96, 97, 98, 99, 100, 101, 102, 103, 104, 105, 106, 107, 108, 109, 110, 111, 112, 113, 114

Commissioning	1
Specific Warning	6
General Warning	37
Completion of Arguments	31
Migration and Cutting Ties	16
Purification and selection	15
Reward and Punishment	2

Medani Surahs

- It's a Makkan Surah.
- It is the 108th Surah of the Quran.
- It is part of Chapter 7 of the Quran, one of its seven chapters.
- It falls within the phase of the Prophet Muhammad's mission when he was asked by God to sever ties with the disbelievers and to await further instructions before migrating.
- This phase is called *"Hijrah wal Bara'a"*.
- After this phase, the punishment was about to start.

Introduction to Surah Al-Kauthar

Relationship between 107 and 108

Surah 107 Crimes of Quraish		Surah 108 Dethroning them due to these crimes

- Surah Al-Maun (107) and Al-Kauthar (108) form a pair. Meaning their subject matter is intrinsically related.
- The first surah (107) mentions the crimes of the leadership of the Quraysh, particularly of Abu Lahab, while the second one (108) declares their removal from the custodianship of the Baytullah because of these crimes. It is evident from their contents that the first one was revealed as the final warning to the Quraysh and the second as great glad tidings of the future in Makkah in the phase of migration and acquittal of the Prophet's mission.
- Surah al-Maun is directed at the Quraysh, and its theme is to inform their leadership, particularly Abu Lahab, of the doom that has been destined for them due to their crimes.
- Surah al-Kawthar is addressed to Prophet Muhammad, and its theme is to give glad tidings that the custodianship of the Baytullah shall now be transferred to him, and his enemies shall be totally routed from the face of the earth.

بِسْمِ اللَّهِ الرَّحْمَنِ الرَّحِيمِ

إِنَّا أَعْطَيْنَاكَ الْكَوْثَرَ فَصَلِّ لِرَبِّكَ وَ انْحَرْ إِنَّ شَانِئَكَ هُوَ الْأَبْتَرُ

[O Prophet!] We have bestowed upon you this abundant good. So, (from now on) pray only for your Lord [in this ancient House] and offer (here) sacrifice only for Him. Undoubtedly, your enemy has no roots, and soon none will remain to remember him. (108: 1-3)

What is Al-Kauthar?

The most common understanding of this word is summarized here:

- **A river or fountain in Paradise:** Many hadith report that the Prophet was given a special river called *Al-Kauthar* in Paradise.

- **Abundance of good:** Some interpreters take it more broadly as "plenty of goodness" — encompassing blessings such as prophethood, the Quran, knowledge, followers, and a spiritual legacy.

- **Lineage/descendants:** A few have linked it to the continuation of the Prophet's progeny through his daughter Fatimah, despite enemies mocking him as "cut off" (الأَبْتَر).

The understanding of Hamid Uddin Farahi

- The actual word is *Al-Kauthar*.

- The true nature of *Al-Kauthar* will be determined by the rights it possesses. The obligations or rights of this *Al-Kauthar* are described immediately in the next verse: "So (from now on) pray only for your Almighty and offer sacrifice from him alone".

- These rights pertain only to the Baytullah, as it is the only place where both of these rituals of worship are combined with full majesty.

- If a person reflects on this verse, he will gather that it is only this place of worship that is a treasure of abundant good for every Muslim, and it is also the metaphorical manifestation of the stream of *Al-Kawthar* that dwellers of Paradise will drink from. This stream too will be given to Prophet Muhammad, as is evident from many narratives.

- What is described in the stream's narrations is actually the spiritual manifestation of the *Baytullah* and its surrounding atmosphere.

The custodianship of Kabaah

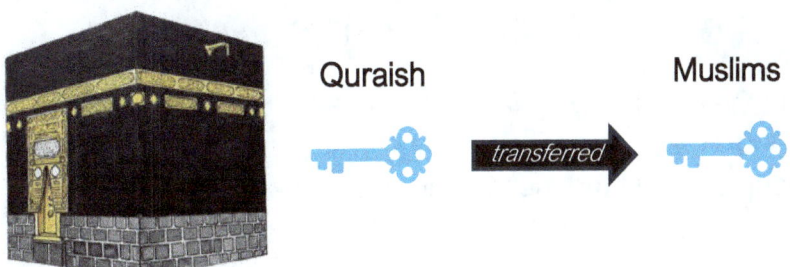

Quraish   Muslims

transferred

- The subject matter of Chapter 7 is to inform Prophet Muhammad and his companions that the final arguments have been presented to the addressees of the Quran, and that it is now time to sever ties with them and migrate. Surah 108 must be read in that context.

- One of the objectives of Prophet Muhammad was to purify the House of God of the filth of polytheism and restore it as the center of monotheism for the entire world, for which it was originally built.

- When the Quran declared that God had granted him the treasure of abundant good, it meant that the Quraysh would be deposed from the political leadership of Arabia, which they had held through their relationship with the House of God, a legacy of the Prophets Ibrahim and Ismael.

- The custodianship of this house would be taken from them and handed to the Prophet and his followers. This constitutes great glad tidings given to him right before his migration to Madinah and acquittal from the disbelievers of his nation.

Who has the custodianship of Kabaah today?

Key rituals dedicated to God

Salah and Sacrifice

1. All Muslims in the world pray by facing towards Kabaah. It is the center of worshiping God.
2. Millions of people pray in the mosque around it throughout the year.
3. Prayers are part of the rituals of Umrah and Hajj, specifically performed in Masjid Al Haram around the Kabaah.
4. Since the time of Prophet Ibrahim, it has been the place where people have sacrificed animals and distributed the meat for charity.
5. During Umrah and Hajj, the ritual of animal sacrifice is also performed in and around Masjid Al-Haram

- After mentioning the blessing of Al-Kauthar bestowed upon the Prophet, God specified the obligations that accompany that gift – Salah and sacrifice must be dedicated to God alone.
- The Quraysh have corrupted both these worship rituals by including their self-made deities in them.
- God instructed Prophet Muhammad that he should cleanse this place from all types of polytheistic practices and religious innovations, and from now on, both Salah and offering sacrifice must be dedicated only to the One God.
- Their prayers were mostly dedicated to the idols placed in the Kabaah, and they used to slaughter sacrifices dedicated to these idols, and sometimes a portion of them.

Glad Tidings for Muslims and a Prophecy Fulfilled

- This Surah also acts as a sign of the Truth of Prophet Muhammad and the Quran. This Surah contains a great prophecy that was fulfilled word for word.
- The Quraish used to propagate the idea that Prophet Muhammad had invented a new religion and had cut ties with his family, culture, and traditions of his forefathers. As a result, no one will remember him, and he will be forgotten because of his "rebellion".
- God made a declaration that soon after this gift is given, his arch enemies will be destroyed, become rootless, and no one will remain alive to even remember their names.

- Within 2-3 years, the entire leadership of Quraish was punished and killed in the Battle of Badr, and no one in Quraish remained alive to remember the names of these leaders.

Assignment

Read Surah Al-Maun and compare its subject matter and content with Surah Al-Kauthar as they make a pair.

Chapter 20

Studying Surah Alam-Nashrah

In this chapter, we will study Surah Alam-Nashrah by applying the principles of understanding the Quran we have studied in this course.

Placement of Surah Alam-Nashrah

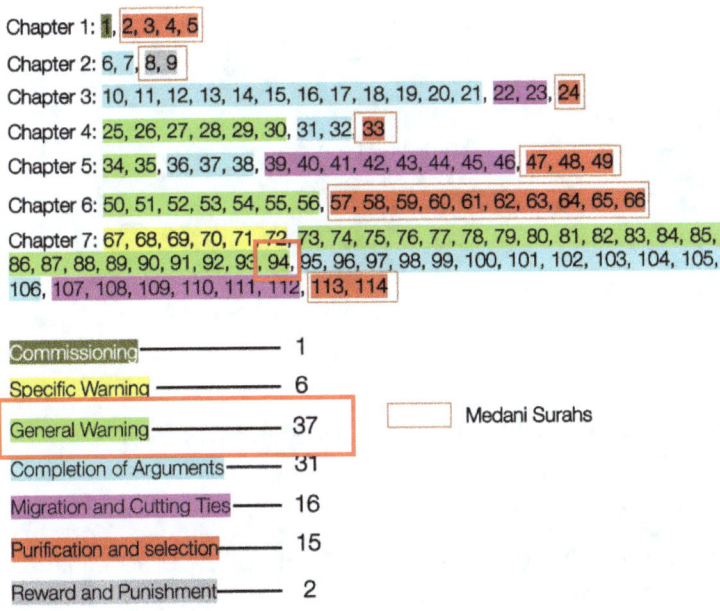

Chapter 1: 1, 2, 3, 4, 5
Chapter 2: 6, 7, 8, 9
Chapter 3: 10, 11, 12, 13, 14, 15, 16, 17, 18, 19, 20, 21, 22, 23, 24
Chapter 4: 25, 26, 27, 28, 29, 30, 31, 32, 33
Chapter 5: 34, 35, 36, 37, 38, 39, 40, 41, 42, 43, 44, 45, 46, 47, 48, 49
Chapter 6: 50, 51, 52, 53, 54, 55, 56, 57, 58, 59, 60, 61, 62, 63, 64, 65, 66
Chapter 7: 67, 68, 69, 70, 71, 72, 73, 74, 75, 76, 77, 78, 79, 80, 81, 82, 83, 84, 85, 86, 87, 88, 89, 90, 91, 92, 93, 94, 95, 96, 97, 98, 99, 100, 101, 102, 103, 104, 105, 106, 107, 108, 109, 110, 111, 112, 113, 114

Commissioning ——————— 1
Specific Warning ——————— 6
General Warning ——————— 37 | | Medani Surahs
Completion of Arguments ——— 31
Migration and Cutting Ties ——— 16
Purification and selection ——— 15
Reward and Punishment ——— 2

- It's a Makkan Surah.
- It is the 94th Surah of the Quran.
- It is part of Chapter 7 of the Quran, one of its seven chapters.
- It falls within the phase of the Prophet Muhammad's mission when he issued a general warning to his direct and indirect addressees and faced the ensuing challenges.
- This phase is called *"Indhaar-e-Aam"*
- After this phase, the final arguments will be given to convince the disbelievers.

Introduction to Surah Alam-Nashrah

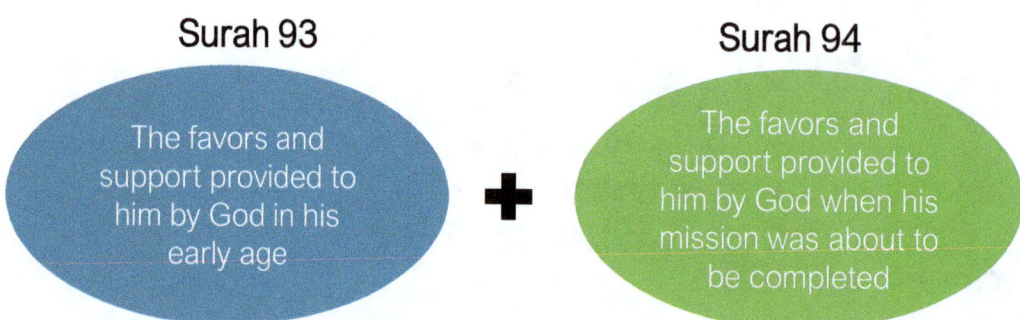

Surah 93

The favors and support provided to him by God in his early age

+

Surah 94

The favors and support provided to him by God when his mission was about to be completed

- Surah Ad-Duha (93) and Alam-Nashrah (94) form a pair. Meaning their subject matter has a deeper relationship.
- This pair is a great example of Quranic coherence.
- This pair is unique as both Surahs directly address the incidents and personal life experiences of the Prophet Muhammad.
- These Surahs specifically console the Prophet's heart in moments of solitude and grief.
- Surah Ad-Duha focuses on God's favors in the past and the bright future ahead.
- Surah Alam-Nashrah focuses on relief from the hardships of current duties and the fruits of perseverance.

بِسْمِ اللَّهِ الرَّحْمَنِ الرَّحِيمِ

اَلَمْ نَشْرَحْ لَكَ صَدْرَكَ ۚ وَ وَضَعْنَا عَنْكَ وِزْرَكَ ۙ الَّذِیْ اَنْقَضَ ظَهْرَكَ ۙ وَ رَفَعْنَا لَكَ ذِكْرَكَ ؕ

فَاِنَّ مَعَ الْعُسْرِ يُسْرًا ۙ اِنَّ مَعَ الْعُسْرِ يُسْرًا ؕ فَاِذَا فَرَغْتَ فَانْصَبْ ۙ وَ اِلٰی رَبِّكَ فَارْغَبْ

Have We not opened up your heart for you [O Prophet]? And have We not relieved you of your burden that was breaking your back? And for your sake, did We not raise your voice (so that the message may reach everyone)? Therefore, [rest assured,] with this difficulty you are now facing, a great ease awaits. With this difficulty, a great ease awaits. So, when you are free from this task, labor hard in worship and remain attached to your Lord with all fervor. (94: 1-8)

God's support in the Prophet's preaching mission

Opening the heart of the Prophet

- It is the understanding and insights that God specially bestowed on the Prophet in matters of religion and its preaching. It is because of this confidence in God that the greatest of opposition did not stumble his determination and resolve.

The burden breaking his back

- This sentence and the one that follows are connected to the first sentence and should be translated accordingly. The burden mentioned in the verse refers to the grief the Prophet experienced before being called to prophethood. First, the grief of trying to find guidance, and then the initial response of his nation after the prophethood was given to him.

Supported his voice and message

- This refers to how his once feeble voice became a reverberating roar throughout all of Arabia. It all started with reaching out to people during Hajj, and subsequently it spread to the far-flung areas of Arabia and then to other regions.

With "every" difficulty, there is ease

- The general understanding among most scholars of verses 5-6 is that there is a universal principle of God: life is a blend of difficulty and ease. However, challenges are always accompanied by relief, either during or after them.
- The word Al-Usr has the definite article, making it specific, whereas Yusr lacks it, making it more generic. This implies that multiple forms of ease accompany a single hardship.
- However, some people do not experience this universal rule and face difficulties one after the other in their lives, with no ease in sight.
- Examining this verse within its broader context (Surah Ad-Duha and Alam-Nashrah), it addresses the situation of the Prophet. Plus, there is word repetition.
- The repetition emphasizes the glad tidings. The period in which this Surah was revealed was apparently a very testing one. God presented various incidents of the Prophet's life to reassure him. He was told that the God Who endowed him with all these blessings was there to help him; very soon, these difficult times would give way to ease; the hindrances in his way would be removed, and he and his companions would finally reach the destination the Almighty had appointed as an established practice for His messengers.
- The words are rather precise here. But in Surah An-Naṣr, details are cited. It is stated that God's help and victory would come, and the Prophet would see people entering the folds of Islam in multitudes.

Glad-tidings and Post-mission Activities

- Found in the word فَرَغْتَ are the glad tidings that he would be able to successfully complete this mission after surmounting all the impediments that came his way.
- The Prophet is told that once the phase of divine support and victory is over and he has fulfilled his responsibility successfully, he should fully devote himself to worshipping the Almighty, because it is only through this effort and devotion that he will reap rewards when he meets his Lord.
- In complying with this final directive, the Prophet began to spend more and more time in worship. Such was the extent of his involvement that he would often feel swelling in his feet due to prolonged standing in prayer.
- A similar message is given in Surah An-Nasr, also in the end.

> The Prophet used to offer night prayers till his feet became swollen. Somebody said to him, "Allah has forgiven you and your faults of the past and those to follow, why do you worship so much?" On that, he said,
>
> أَفَلاَ أَكُونُ عَبْدًا شَكُورًا
>
> "Shouldn't I be a thankful slave of Allah?"

Assignment

> Read Surah Ad-Duha and compare its subject matter and content with Surah Alam-Nashrah as they make a pair.

Chapter 21

Studying Surah Al-Asr

In this chapter, we will study Surah Al-Asr by applying the principles of understanding the Quran we have studied in this course.

Placement of Surah Al-Asr

Chapter 1: 1, 2, 3, 4, 5
Chapter 2: 6, 7, 8, 9
Chapter 3: 10, 11, 12, 13, 14, 15, 16, 17, 18, 19, 20, 21, 22, 23, 24
Chapter 4: 25, 26, 27, 28, 29, 30, 31, 32, 33
Chapter 5: 34, 35, 36, 37, 38, 39, 40, 41, 42, 43, 44, 45, 46, 47, 48, 49
Chapter 6: 50, 51, 52, 53, 54, 55, 56, 57, 58, 59, 60, 61, 62, 63, 64, 65, 66
Chapter 7: 67, 68, 69, 70, 71, 72, 73, 74, 75, 76, 77, 78, 79, 80, 81, 82, 83, 84, 85, 86, 87, 88, 89, 90, 91, 92, 93, 94, 95, 96, 97, 98, 99, 100, 101, 102, 103, 104, 105, 106, 107, 108, 109, 110, 111, 112, 113, 114

Commissioning	1
Specific Warning	6
General Warning	37
Completion of Arguments	31
Migration and Cutting Ties	16
Purification and selection	15
Reward and Punishment	2

☐ Medani Surahs

- It's a Makkan Surah.
- It is the 103rd Surah of the Quran.
- It is part of Chapter 7 of the Quran, one of its seven chapters.
- It falls within the phase of the Prophet Muhammad's mission when he presented the final argument before being asked to migrate.
- This phase is called *"Itmaam al-Hujjah".*
- After this phase, the Muslims were asked to cut ties and migrate.

Introduction to Surah Al-Asr

Surah 103

The law of retribution of God in this world

Surah 104

Warning to Quraish based on that law of retribution

- Surah Al-Asr (103) and Al-Humazah (104) form a pair. Meaning their subject matter has a deeper relationship.
- Both Surahs are directed at the leadership of the Quraysh. It is evident from their subject matter that they were revealed in Makkah, a little before the Prophet Muhammad's migration to Madinah, during the phase of *Itmam al-Hujjah* of his preaching mission.
- The theme of Surah Al-Asr is to validate the law of retribution, which the Quraysh would now encounter in accordance with the verdict delivered by the divine court of justice.
- The theme of Surah Al-Humazah is to warn, with reference to this law, the leadership of the Quraysh of their fate. These leaders were afflicted with the conceit of their wealth and were adamant in showing a rebellious, slanderous, and contemptuous attitude towards the Prophet.

بِسْمِ اللَّهِ الرَّحْمَٰنِ الرَّحِيمِ

Wal-Asr → Swear-by
Rest of the verses → Swear-for

وَ الْعَصْرِ

اِنَّ الْاِنْسَانَ لَفِیْ خُسْرٍ اِلَّا الَّذِیْنَ اٰمَنُوْا وَ عَمِلُوا الصّٰلِحٰتِ وَ تَوَاصَوْا بِالْحَقِّ ۬ وَ تَوَاصَوْا بِالصَّبْرِ

Time (history) bears witness that <u>these people</u> shall definitely be in a state of loss. Yes, except those who professed faith, did righteous deeds, and urged one another to the truth, and urged one another to remain steadfast on the truth. (103: 1-3)

Oath of 'Time'

- Time here refers to the <u>complete period of prophethood, from Adam to Muhammad,</u> which bears witness.
- In this period, the court of justice was set up on earth for the immediate addressees of the messengers of God, and the rebellious among them were the losers.
- The Quran presents the historical evidence from the accounts of Aad, the Thamud, the people of Noah, Lot, and Shoaib, as well as other similar stories. This evidence is presented here in one word (the Time). In fact, this is the evidence of the lesser days of judgement on the greater Day of Judgement.
- These lesser days of judgment were brought about to validate the greater day, much like scientific facts are experimentally validated in a laboratory. Besides the evidence found in the world around human beings to substantiate the Day of Judgment, there is also historical evidence that supports this concept.
- It is also evident that only those were saved from this punishment who accepted the faith and did righteous deeds.
- This practice of God with the Messengers and their nations will not change.

The word Al-Insaan with Alif-Laam

- The word الْأِنْسَان is not generic in nature. The *Alif Lam* affixed to it defines it, and the reference is to the addressees of Muhammad, to whom the truth was conclusively communicated, and in spite of this, they persisted in their arrogance.
- Loss here refers to loss both in this world and the next. In other words, they will be punished in this world like the other foremost addressees of other messengers of God were, and a great torment awaits them in the Hereafter.
- They have their eyes fixed on high status, power, and the wealth of this world. They believe that opposing the Prophet will earn them a lucrative deal. In reality, they are facing the law of retribution and will soon reach their fate. Hence, they should remain aware that if they persist in this attitude, they will ultimately lose.

The recipe for safety from retribution in this world and the next

Note: It is interesting to note that the recipe for safety mentioned here is not only applicable to the people addressed here, but also to all Muslims until the Day of Judgment.

- These verses outline the individual and collective obligations imposed on a person, as well as the requirements for his eternal salvation.
- The message conveyed by 114 Surahs is succinctly stated in three verses of this Surah.
- Imam Shafi'i stated that reflecting on Surah Al-Asr will suffice for them.

1   EEMAN

- If something is accepted with the certitude of the heart, then this is called *Eeman*.
- This faith or *Eeman* consists of five things:
    - Belief in God
    - Belief in the Angels
    - Belief in the Prophets
    - Belief in Divine Books
    - Belief in the Day of Judgement

2   RIGHTEOUS DEEDS

- The mention of righteous deeds after faith serves to explain faith.
- It is this very essence of faith on account of which the Quran demands from a person that, besides substantiation from the heart, his words and deeds should also testify to it. Thus, it calls every act of virtue emanating from Eeman an essential quality of a believer.
- It is evident from this that both faith and righteous deeds are essential to one another. Thus, just as righteous deeds are necessary for faith, faith is necessary for righteous deeds.

True Eeman

3 COUNSELLING ONE ANOTHER AND REMAINING PATIENT ON THAT

- This is the obligation of preaching that the Quran has imposed on all its followers, with no exception.

- Humans do not merely live in isolation; they are also members of a family or citizens of a society. Thus, on this basis, he is directed here not to remain negligent of the betterment of his surroundings.

- This obligation is mentioned as a part of righteous deeds as their explanation, because this is a natural requirement of one's love for the truth. A person is very vehement in wanting others to love what they themselves love.

- The word تَوَاصَوْا suggests that the circle of this preaching is one's own immediate surroundings and relationships. Thus, the preacher and the preached are not distinct from one another. Every person acts as both a preacher and an addressee to this preaching at all times.

- The words حَقّ and صَبْر mentioned in the verse need deliberation. God did not say: "they urged others to righteous deeds." On the contrary, His words are: "they urged one another to the truth and urged one another to remain steadfast on it."

A believer <u>must do all four things</u> if they seek guaranteed eternal salvation

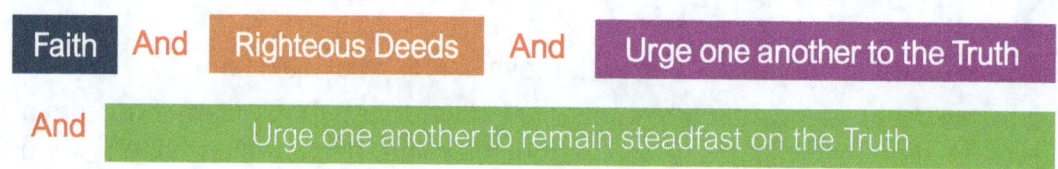

Faith | And | Righteous Deeds | And | Urge one another to the Truth

And | Urge one another to remain steadfast on the Truth

Discuss and highlight how you can practice the teachings of Surah Al-Asr in your life.